SpringerBriefs in Business

More information about this series at http://www.springer.com/series/8860

Ludovica Cesareo

Counterfeiting and Piracy

A Comprehensive Literature Review

Springer

Ludovica Cesareo
The Wharton School
University of Pennsylvania
Philadelphia, PA
USA

ISSN 2191-5482 ISSN 2191-5490 (electronic)
SpringerBriefs in Business
ISBN 978-3-319-25356-5 ISBN 978-3-319-25357-2 (eBook)
DOI 10.1007/978-3-319-25357-2

Library of Congress Control Number: 2015955392

Springer Cham Heidelberg New York Dordrecht London

Printed on acid-free paper

Springer International Publishing AG Switzerland is part of Springer Science+Business Media
(www.springer.com)

To Prof. Pastore, to Alberto.
For believing in me since the first day,
and continuing to do so every day since.

Foreword

This book presents some of the results of the scientific research Ludovica conducted while doing her Ph.D. at the Management Department of Sapienza University of Rome. Having worked as her advisor throughout this whole period, it is for me a source of great pride to present this excellent work to those who want to dedicate some (well-spent) time reading it. I will examine this work with a novel approach, by looking at several different aspects that I believe to be key for our profession. I have identified these aspects through my important experience as the President of the Italian Society of Management (Società Italiana di Management—SIMA), the Scientific Society of the Italian Professors of Management.

As a Scientific Society, one of the important issues we are tackling is to try to stir the revision of evaluation systems toward a more accurate direction, while also suggesting to young scholars who are taking their first steps in their careers some guidelines for a correct interpretation of their job. The mantra of this approach can thus be expressed as follows: the job of a management professor must be interpreted with A.R.R.T.E (*A/N—in Italian the word 'arte' means 'art'*), which is the acronym for amplitude (in the sense of openness), rigor, relevance, transfer, and ethics. Particular attention must therefore be given to:

– Amplitude: which, in the sense of openness, means participating, on one hand,—to the national and international scientific debate and operating in interdisciplinary and inter-university research teams; on the other hand, it means developing a concrete and fruitful collaboration with companies, the territory, institutions, and society at large, and participating in the socioeconomic debate among all these actors.
– Rigor: do quality research, adopting rigorous methodologies from a scientific point of view.
– Relevance: produce real, practical benefits for companies and society, generating knowledge as a competitive resource.
– Transfer: strive for knowledge transfer to the different target audiences (managers, students, institutions, etc.), using the most appropriate channels.

– Ethics: carry out the job conscientiously, following the principles of professional ethics in research, teaching, and other activities.

Now, to provide a brief and unusual presentation, let us try to use this scheme, which should be used for the job of professor in its entirety, to the specific context of this book.

Amplitude (openness). The book is based on research that Ludovica has carried out on the subject of counterfeiting over three years. Such research has been conducted in collaboration with other scholars, including two of the leading experts worldwide on the topic: Peggy Chaudhry (Villanova University) and Barbara Stöttinger (Vienna University). Therefore, excellent Amplitude!

Rigor. The study was conducted very rigorously, in accordance with the strict content analysis methodology proposed for the literature reviews. It is a very thorough work that embraces a 35-year time span, from the actual emergence of the counterfeiting problem to today. The body of the literature collected and analyzed is truly remarkable: as many as 572 articles (572!), published in 169 journals. Absolute Rigor!

Relevance. The theme of the work revolves around the counterfeiting and piracy phenomenon, i.e., the unauthorized copying of trademarks, copyrighted works, or patented inventions. It is an issue of extraordinary importance, both in virtue of the size of the phenomenon and the implications for institutions, companies, and consumers. The International Chamber of Commerce (ICC) estimates the value of unauthorized copying of trademarks, copyrighted works, and patented inventions, or the unauthorized use of someone else's legitimately registered trademark, to be worth about $1.7 trillion. The affected sectors are quite diverse: clothing and accessories, food, audiovisual material, electrical and electronic computer equipment, watches and jewelry, perfumes and cosmetics, auto parts, and all the way to toys and pharmaceuticals. As the work clearly shows, the negative effects of counterfeiting are spread across several levels. At a high, public level, it has an impact on legality, the prosperity of the economy, national tax revenues, and employment. For the companies that are its victims, counterfeiting impacts on turnover, profitability, and brand image and undermines investments in innovation. Finally, for consumers, a counterfeit product may constitute a fraud and, especially in certain sectors, a health hazard. We derive that studying the phenomenon and identifying the managerial guidelines to mitigate its effects is an extraordinarily relevant activity.

Transfer. Sometimes scientific research tends to be auto-referential, either for the object under scrutiny, or the methods, languages, and channels used. It is not the case with this work. The research addresses a topic of interest to a wide audience; it is presented through a succinct, clear, easily comprehensible monograph that dedicates a wide section to the managerial implications; it is published through a prestigious international publishing house. Great Transfer!

Ethics. The research topic itself is of ethical relevance, as well as the contributions that the work gives to tackling the counterfeiting problem. As a side note, the approach taken by the Author—which is always impeccable—throughout her research activity and beyond is an excellent example of ethics.

Therefore, I can certainly say that this is a work of ARTTE (*art*) and that it constitutes, without a doubt, an essential point of reference both for anyone conducting research on this topic and for the institutions and companies facing the phenomenon. All that is left to do is take advantage of it, and delve into the reading.

Let me conclude with a personal thought: It is wonderful to see this stage of Ludovica's professional development completed! And what a great satisfaction to note, once again, the standards of excellence that distinguish her work!

Fly Ludovica, fly!

September 2015

Alberto Pastore
Sapienza University of Rome

Acknowledgments

This work stems from my doctoral dissertation at Sapienza University of Rome, a wonderful three-year journey completed in December 2014. If today, nine months later, I am able to publish this book as a Postdoc at Wharton, it is due to some wonderful people, whom I wish to thank.

To Prof. Alberto Pastore, wise advisor and friend throughout all of my academic career, thank you for your continuous support and encouragement. This book is published because of your spur, even from far away.

To Prof. Peggy Chaudhry and Prof. Barbara Stöttinger, co-authors in much of my prior and current work, thank you for sharing your immense knowledge with me and for always treating me as a par. We are the official 'counterfeiting ladies' dream team!

To my Mother and my Brother, thank you for your support, emotional and practical, throughout my Ph.D.

To all the people who are an important part of my life, thank you. You are all in my heart and mind, and this work has been completed also thanks to you.

Finally, to Pitou, my source of inspiration and motivation, thank you for your love, patience, kindness, enthusiasm, encouragement, and infinite support every step of the way.

Contents

Chapter 1
Introduction

Abstract The purpose of this chapter is to introduce the counterfeiting and piracy phenomena and to illustrate the purpose of the book. After delving into what illicit trade is, the chapter highlights which industries are affected the most by it, what the numbers of the phenomena are on an international level, the typologies of counterfeit and pirated products, and the main distribution channels. It then gives a brief overview of the academic research on the topic over the past few decades and goes on to put forth the objectives of the volume. Finally, it outlines the structure of the remaining chapters.

Keywords Counterfeiting · Piracy · Illicit trade · Literature review · Intellectual property rights (IPRs) · Industries

Counterfeiting and piracy are persistent, widespread, global phenomena that have challenged managers and scholars for a long time. The latest estimate from the International Chamber of Commerce (ICC) indicates that the total global value of counterfeiting and piracy could reach a staggering peak of $1.7 trillion by the end of 2015 (Economics 2011). Since trademarks have been used fraudulently to both deceive consumers and satisfy their aspirational, status-seeking purchases, the ease with which electronic data can be copied and distributed through the Internet has led to an epidemic of piracy. As a result, counterfeiting and piracy have drawn considerable attention from scholars, while causing significant angst for managers (Bush et al. 1989; Yang et al. 2004; Berman 2008; Wilcock and Boys 2014).

No company is immune to counterfeiting and piracy: while infringers previously focused on the most lucrative markets, such as consumer electronics, luxury products, apparel and accessories, optical media and pharmaceuticals, over the last two decades these illegal practices have expanded to include virtually every industry, from fake foods and beverages to books, from mobile phone batteries to toys.[1] The latest European Commission Report (2014)[2] highlights how, in 2013, the

---

[1]UNICRI and Bascap (2013). Confiscation of the Proceeds of IP Crime A modern tool for deterring counterfeiting and piracy. Report, p. 9.

[2]European Commission (2014). Report on EU customs enforcement of intellectual property rights. Results at the EU border 2013.

L. Cesareo, *Counterfeiting and Piracy*,
SpringerBriefs in Business, DOI 10.1007/978-3-319-25357-2_1

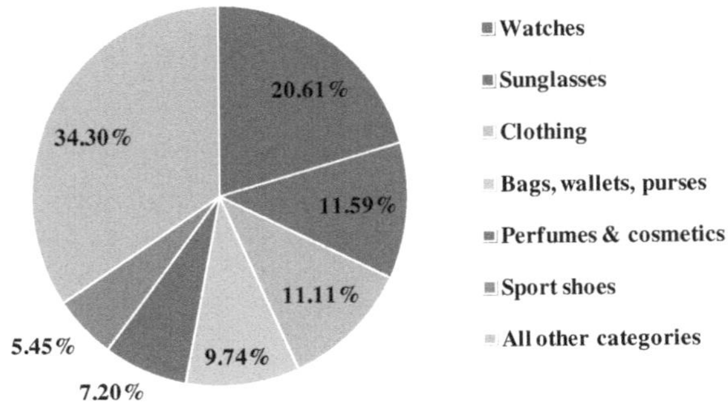

Fig. 1.1 Counterfeit and pirated goods seized at the EU border (2013) by category, in terms equivalent of domestic retail value (DRV) (%)

EU customs agencies opened almost 87.000 cases for a total of about 36 million illicit goods whose domestic retail value (DRV—i.e., the price at which they would have been sold on the national market if they had been genuine) was worth almost €768 million. The most affected industries (in terms of lost equivalent DRV) were the fashion and luxury goods industries that between accessories (watches, sunglasses, bags, wallet, purses) and clothing comprised 53.05 % of the total (Fig. 1.1).

Counterfeiting and piracy, while often used as synonyms in the academic literature, refer to two distinct aspects of the same phenomenon, i.e. the "unauthorized copying of patented inventions, copyrighted works or trademarks" (Harvey 1988, p. 19), or more simply, the violation of Intellectual Property Rights (IPRs). Specifically, counterfeiting refers to the "unauthorized use of someone else's legitimately registered trademark" while piracy refers to "the violation of someone else's copyright" (Cordell et al. 1996). Therefore, while counterfeiting regards the copying of physical products and brands, piracy regards the illegal reproduction of intellectual, content products, such as music, movies, software or print, even though the two concepts are treated similarly by the reference literature (Harvey 1987).

The spectrum of counterfeit products ranges from high-quality counterfeits (that look just like the original and use, illegitimately, the legitimate brand name), to look-alikes (knockoffs that duplicate the original product bearing a different brand name), to shoddy, low quality, unconvincing imitations[3] (Harvey 1987). Therefore, based upon the quality of the replica, counterfeiting can be either *deceptive* or *non-deceptive* (Grossman and Shapiro 1988): in the former, the buyer is deceived into believing that the good they are obtaining is the real thing; in the latter, sometimes called 'piracy' in the literature (hence the confusion upon the definitions—Phau et al. 2001), consumers choose the fake alternative willingly, becoming 'accomplices' of the counterfeiters.

[3]An additional typology of illegal goods, that are not strictly counterfeits, are the so called 'gray-market goods' or 'overruns', which are legitimate, original products distributed through unauthorized channels (McDonald and Roberts 1994; Hilton et al. 2004). The academic literature often overlaps the two domains.

Counterfeiting and piracy hit many different product categories: luxury goods, fashion goods (apparel and accessories), CDs and DVDs, computer software, cigarettes, precious stones, toys, credit cards, auto and airplane parts, convenience goods (baby formulas, shampoo, toothpaste, condoms, etc.), fertilizers and pesticides, medical devices and pharmaceuticals, etc. (Chapa et al. 2006). Unauthorized products are usually distributed through offline channels, such as street vendors, flea markets or malls. This traditional commercialization requires a physical proximity between the seller and the buyer, in a sense limiting, at least physically, the uncontrolled spread of illicit goods. However, the advent of the Internet and of digital technologies (peer-to-peer—P2P—networks) has fostered the online distribution of counterfeit goods and the illegal sharing and downloading of content goods, so to tenfold the proportions of the phenomena (Robertson et al. 2012). In addition, given that content, information goods (such as music, movies and software) in the digital format share two characteristics of public goods (they are non-rivalrous and non-excludable[4]), the phenomena cannot seem to be stemmed (Sinha and Mandel 2008).

It is widely acknowledged that research on counterfeiting and piracy is of vital interest to different groups: governmental entities, companies and consumers. Governmental entities view counterfeiting and piracy as detrimental occurrences to development, gross domestic product (GDP), labor, and income from tax revenues. Managers are interested in the topic since counterfeiting and piracy of their products reduce revenues, tarnish brand image and cut investments. Consumers need to acknowledge the existence, the negative consequences of and the risks that the purchase of a counterfeit/pirated good generate for themselves and for society overall. As a result, researchers consider counterfeiting and piracy as challenging areas that need to be further explored in order to find possible solutions to such harmful incidents.

Perhaps unfortunately, the academic literature on counterfeiting and piracy is replete with studies that have addressed different, often niche and separate, aspects of the phenomena. These are: (1) overall descriptions of counterfeiting and piracy; (2) the international and national legal frameworks and organizations put in place to govern them; (3) consumer behavior analyses, in terms of theoretical domains and determinants of attitudes, intentions and actual purchase behaviors; (4) effects of counterfeiting and piracy, both negative and, sometimes, positive, on legitimate companies; (5) managerial strategies, tools and actions employed by companies in response to the phenomena; and (6) superficial looks at the supply of unauthorized products, through studies on the infringers' supply and distribution chains (Staake et al. 2009). Among these works, the most tested product categories are physical products (mostly fashion, high quality, luxury goods; content products: CDs, DVDs, Software CDs) plus their digital versions (online distribution through P2P

[4]Non-rivalry implies that the consumption of a product by one user does not reduce the ability of others to consume the same product; non-excludability implies that it is not possible to prevent others from consuming the same good by paying for it.

networks or illegal downloading of content, information goods—music, movies, software). The result of all these contributions is a fragmented, diverse and often inconsistent literature that lacks a coherent underlying structure. Consequently, there is a need to synthesize the extant knowledge on counterfeiting and piracy in order to facilitate the understanding of the phenomena while also helping managers in their everyday struggles against them.

This book examines the existing body of literature on counterfeiting and piracy over a 35-year time span (1980–2015), in order to assess the current state of the art. The 1980s were chosen as a starting point since it is believed that the globalization of markets began around that time (Levitt 1983) and articles regarding counterfeiting and piracy, global phenomena, were beginning to be published in the academic literature.

The main objectives of this book are *to analyze and categorize previous studies in order to highlight the main figures and trends in scientific research on counterfeiting and piracy, and identify theoretical gaps and paths for future research. The central contribution of this book is that it provides the most comprehensive, interdisciplinary view to date on the state of research on counterfeiting and piracy.*

The rest of the book is structured as follows. Chapter 2 provides a brief overview of past literature reviews on counterfeiting and piracy. Chapter 3 describes the methodology followed for the main analyses. Chapters 4 and 5 present the results of the content analysis of the counterfeiting and piracy literature and its evolution over time. Specifically, Chap. 4 focuses on the figures and trends in the literature (highlighting the main typologies of studies, methodologies, authors, citations, products and study contexts, with a separate focus for both quantitative and qualitative empirical studies) while Chap. 5 focuses on the classification of prior literature (categorizing the articles based upon the main themes emerging from the content analysis). Chapter 6 discusses the critical insights deriving from both the descriptive and content analyses, provides the managerial implications, and discusses some of the most recent research that tries to tackle emerging gaps in the literature. Finally, in Chap. 7, after walking through some of the limitations of the methodological approach, the conclusions offer suggestions about the future of the counterfeiting and piracy literature by providing some paths for the further developments of these fields.

References

Berman B (2008) Strategies to detect and reduce counterfeiting activity. Bus Horiz 51(3):191–199. doi:10.1016/j.bushor.2008.01.002.

Bush RF, Bloch PH, Dawson S (1989) Remedies for product counterfeiting. Bus Horiz 32(1): 59–65.

Chapa S, Minor MS, Maldonado C (2006) Product category and origin effects on consumer responses to counterfeits. J Int Consum Mark 18(4):79–99. doi:10.1300/J046v18n04_05.

Cordell VV, Wongtada N, Kieschnick RL Jr (1996) Counterfeit purchase intentions: role of lawfulness attitudes and product traits as determinants. J Bus Res 35(1):41–53.

Economics F (2011) Estimating the global economic and social impacts of counterfeiting and piracy. A report commissioned by business action to stop counterfeiting and piracy (BASCAP), An ICC Initiative.

Grossman GM, Shapiro C (1988) Foreign counterfeiting of status goods: national bureau of economic research Cambridge. Mass, USA.

Harvey MG (1987) Industrial product counterfeiting: problems and proposed solutions. J Bus Ind Mark 2(4):5–13.

Harvey M (1988) A new way to combat product counterfeiting. Bus Horiz 31(4):19–28.

Hilton B, Choi CJ, Chen S (2004) The ethics of counterfeiting in the fashion industry: quality, credence and profit issues. J Bus Ethics 55(4):343–352.

Levitt T (1983) The globalization of markets. Harvard Bus Rev 61(3):92–102.

McDonald G, Roberts C (1994) Product piracy: the problem that will not go away. J Prod Brand Manage 3(4):55–65.

Phau I, Prendergast G, & Hing Chuen L (2001). Profiling brand-piracy-prone consumers: An exploratory study in Hong Kong's clothing industry. J Fashion Market and Manage: Int J, 5 (1):45–55. doi:10.1108/EUM0000000007278.

Robertson K, McNeill L, Green J, Roberts C (2012) Illegal downloading, ethical concern, and illegal behavior. J Bus Ethics 108(2):215–227.

Sinha RK, Mandel N (2008) Preventing digital music piracy: the carrot or the stick? J Mark 72 (1):1–15.

Staake T, Thiesse F, Fleisch E (2009) The emergence of counterfeit trade: a literature review. Eur J Mark 43(3/4):320–349. doi:10.1108/03090560910935451.

Wilcock AE, Boys KA (2014) Reduce product counterfeiting: an integrated approach. Bus Horiz 57(2):279–288.

Yang D, Sonmez M, Bosworth D (2004) Intellectual property abuses: how should multinationals respond? Long Range Plan 37(5):459–475. doi:10.1016/j.lrp.2004.07.009.

Chapter 2
The Complexity of the Counterfeiting and Piracy Phenomena: A 1980–2015 Literature Review

Abstract The purpose of this chapter is to highlight the results of prior literature reviews on counterfeiting and piracy. These have addressed Intellectual Property Rights (IPRs), counterfeiting (in general and with a focus on luxury goods), and piracy (specifically of music, film and software). The analysis of such contributions highlights the theoretical and practical gap that is then filled in the remainder of the volume.

Keywords Literature reviews · Counterfeiting · Piracy · Intellectual property rights (IPRs) · Categorization

Counterfeiting and piracy are cross-disciplinary academic topics that have been examined by researchers in a variety of fields, from marketing to law, from management to psychology. The literature has always accepted the conceptual overlap between the two domains: results from counterfeiting studies have been extended to piracy studies and vice versa, mostly because companies often tend to protect their products and assets under either of the Intellectual Property Rights (IPRs). While there have been prior literature reviews on the topics, they have either addressed the two issues separately or focused only on a certain aspect of one of the two phenomena, in terms of subjects involved, distribution channels or products/industries tested (*IPRs:* Candelin-Palmqvist et al. 2012; *Counterfeiting*: Eisend and Schuchert-Güler 2006; Staake et al. 2009; Wiedmann et al. 2012; *Piracy*: Kariithi 2011; Goode 2012). Candelin-Palmqvist et al. (2012) review the literature on IPRs in innovation management research, with a minor focus on trademark, copyright, counterfeiting and piracy. Eisend and Schuchert-Güler (2006) review prior literature delving into consumers' attitudes and intentions towards counterfeit goods and suggest a framework to summarize antecedents, moderators and consequences of action based upon four factors: personal, product-related, social/cultural, and situational. Staake et al. (2009), in an extensive literature review on counterfeit trade, categorize prior research into six thematic categories in order to highlight existing research gaps. While clearly stating the intention to focus solely on counterfeit physical goods, thus excluding pirated goods, digital goods and gray-market goods (p. 322), the authors review both counterfeiting and piracy papers, blurring the

L. Cesareo, *Counterfeiting and Piracy*,
SpringerBriefs in Business, DOI 10.1007/978-3-319-25357-2_2

scope of their contribution. Wiedmann et al. (2012) discuss studies that have addressed consumer perceptions of counterfeit luxury goods, highlighting the individual, social, economic and functional evaluations of the product by final consumers and the economic, legal and ethical countermeasures firms can employ to deter demand. Kariithi (2011) reviews extant literature on music, film and software piracy, both physical and digital, putting the accent on the most tested theoretical frameworks and the most employed methodologies of analysis, while Goode (2012), through a rigorous content analysis, reviews the literature solely on digital piracy, highlight six gaps that yet need to be filled.

No prior effort has therefore addressed counterfeiting and piracy as an *unicum*, with a thorough analysis into the most employed methodologies of analysis, the most studied affected industries and product categories, the different sample types involved and the distribution channels (offline and online) used to vehicle counterfeit and pirated goods to the market. To fill such gaps, *the objective of this volume is to provide an extended literature review on both counterfeiting and piracy, of physical and intellectual products, with student and non-student adult samples, qualitative and quantitative methodologies, offline and online, through the analysis of scholarly academic research papers published over the past* 35 *years* (1980–2015). The goal is to highlight the wealth of prior literature while understanding the gaps that still need to be filled in the research on both the counterfeiting and piracy phenomena.

References

Candelin-Palmqvist, H., Sandberg, B., & Mylly, U.-M. (2012). Intellectual property rights in innovation management research: a review. *Technovation, 32*(9–10), 502–512. doi:10.1016/j.technovation.2012.01.005.

Eisend, M., & Schuchert-Güler, P. (2006). Explaining counterfeit purchases: a review and preview. *Acad Mark Sci Rev, 12*(6), 1–25.

Goode, S. (2012). Initial findings of a gap analysis of the digital piracy literature: six undiscovered countries. *J Res Interact Mark, 6*(4), 238–259. doi:10.1108/17505931211282382.

Kariithi, N. K. (2011). Is the devil in the data? A literature review of piracy around the world. *J World Intellect Property, 14*(2), 133–154. doi:10.1111/j.1747-1796.2010.00412.x.

Staake, T., Thiesse, F., & Fleisch, E. (2009). The emergence of counterfeit trade: a literature review. *Eur J Mark, 43*(3/4), 320–349. doi:10.1108/03090560910935451.

Wiedmann, K.-P., Hennigs, N., & Klarmann, C. (2012). Luxury consumption in the trade-off between genuine and counterfeit goods: what are the consumers' underlying motives and value-based drivers? *J Brand Manage, 19*(7), 544–566. doi:10.1057/bm.2012.10.

Chapter 3
Research Methodology

Abstract The purpose of this chapter is to explain the research methodology employed to analyze the existent literature on counterfeiting and piracy. Following some of the leading literature reviews published in top journals, the Author went through an iterating process that started with the main key words, moved onto article selection, skimming and retention/exclusion. The final data set comprised 572 articles published in 169 journals.

Keywords Methodology · Selection · Journal · Counterfeit · Piracy

In order to give the most comprehensive view possible of the counterfeiting and piracy phenomena the focus was placed upon a 35-year time span (1980–2015).[1] To carry out the literature review, the Author followed the recommendations given by Webster and Watson (2002); in addition, different methodologies used by some top literature reviews published in '*The International Journal of Management Reviews*'[2] were also employed (Furrer et al. 2008; Srivastava 2007; Zou and Stan 1998). Finally, we find the most resemblance with the procedures followed by Lehnert et al. (2015), in their research note and review of the empirical ethical decision-making literature.

3.1 Journals and Articles Selection Process

The analysis started with an extensive research in online databases (Ebsco-Host, ABI/ProQuest, Google Scholar, Scopus) with an 'or' criteria between the key words '*Counterfeit*' and '*Piracy*' in the title, the abstract or the key words. Since coun-

[1]The year 2015 was also included in the analyses given the number of contributions already published on the topics as of September, even though the Author acknowledges that further publications will be coming out as the year unravels to the end.
[2]Such journal was chosen as a point of reference since it is one of the only top—ranked journal (Impact factor: 3.857) that publishes literature reviews from different fields, from international and strategic management to organizational behavior, from information systems to marketing.

L. Cesareo, *Counterfeiting and Piracy*,
SpringerBriefs in Business, DOI 10.1007/978-3-319-25357-2_3

terfeiting and piracy do not constitute a stand-alone research discipline, but rather pertain to interdisciplinary fields and can be studied from multiple perspectives, there was no a priori selection of single disciplinary areas (i.e., marketing vs. management) or journals to analyze (i.e., only top ranked 'A' or 'B' journals). Once a substantial number of articles were collected, a second round of research was conducted based upon the main key words cited in the collected literature[3] (n = 66) (Table 3.1).

As mentioned earlier, counterfeiting and piracy are global, interdisciplinary phenomena; therefore, in order to capture the breadth of research on the topics, journals belonging to different fields were selected: business, economics, ethics, information systems, law, management, marketing, operations, psychology and sociology.

The results were therefore filtered for journal name: only articles published in journals belonging to one of the above-mentioned categories were retained for analysis. A total of 702 articles were collected.[4] Each article was then read to verify the affinity with the research objective: 130 articles were discarded since they either misused the words 'counterfeit' or 'piracy' (i.e., piracy in the seas), discussed an area of counterfeiting/piracy not relevant for the chosen objectives (i.e. counterfeit currency) or simply had the wrong focus. In addition, articles that were paragraph-long extracts and not full articles (such as certain contributions in the "*Intellectual Property & Technology Law Journal*—IPTLJ" or the "*Communications of the ACM*—CACM") were also excluded. The final data-set comprised 169 journals and 572 articles. Figure 3.1 shows the number of journals and articles per disciplinary area: the greatest number of contributions can be found in the 'Marketing' (49 journals, 166 articles), 'Business and Management' (45 journals, 132 articles), 'Law, Ethics and Criminology' (15 journals, 101 articles) and 'Operations and Information Systems' (24 journals, 77 articles) areas.

Table 3.2 provides the total list of journals analyzed and the number of articles per journal, in contributions order. The journals that have published the most articles on counterfeiting and piracy are the '*Journal of Business Ethics*' (57 articles), '*Advances in Consumer Research*' (26 articles), '*Business Horizons*' (19 articles), '*Communications of the ACM*' (18 articles), *Review of Economic Research on Copyright Issues* (12 articles), '*The Journal of Consumer Marketing*' (14 articles), the '*Journal of Business Research*' (13 articles), the '*Review of Economic Research on Copyright Issues*' (12 articles), the '*Intellectual Property and Technology Law Journal*' (11 articles), and the '*European Journal of Law and Economics*' (10 articles).

---

[3]Key words that were used only once were excluded from further research since they would have reduced the reliability of the analysis.

[4]In order to avoid an unwieldy corpus and obtain a rigorous academic work, only scholarly research articles were retained for analysis, while conference articles, working papers, book reviews, industry updates and press articles were excluded. Exceptions were made for articles of particular relevance to the body of knowledge that were published either in journals not belonging to the selected fields or in conference proceedings; these were placed in the category 'Other' (n.a.).

Table 3.1 Keywords list

Keywords			
Anti-counterfeiting	Crime	Grounded theory	Neutralization theory
Anti-piracy	Culture	Imitation	Non-deceptive counterfeiting
Attitude	Demographics	Information goods	Patents
Authenticity	Deterrence	Innovation	Perceived risk
Bootlegging	Digital goods	Intellectual property rights (IPRs)	Perceptions
Brand	Digital piracy	Intention to buy	Pricing
Brand protection	Distribution	Internet/ICT	Self-monitoring
Conspicuous consumption	DMCA	Luxury goods	SEM
Consumer behavior	Downloading	Market research	Social identity
Consumer complicity	DRM	Marketing	Software piracy
Consumer ethics	Enforcement	Materialism	TPB
Consumers	Ethics	Morality	TRA
Copyright	Factor analysis	Motivation	Trademarks
Counterfeit goods	Fashion	Movie piracy	Vertical segmentation
Counterfeit luxury goods	File sharing/peer-to-peer	Music piracy	Willingness to pay
Country-of-origin	Game theory	Network effects/externalities	WOM

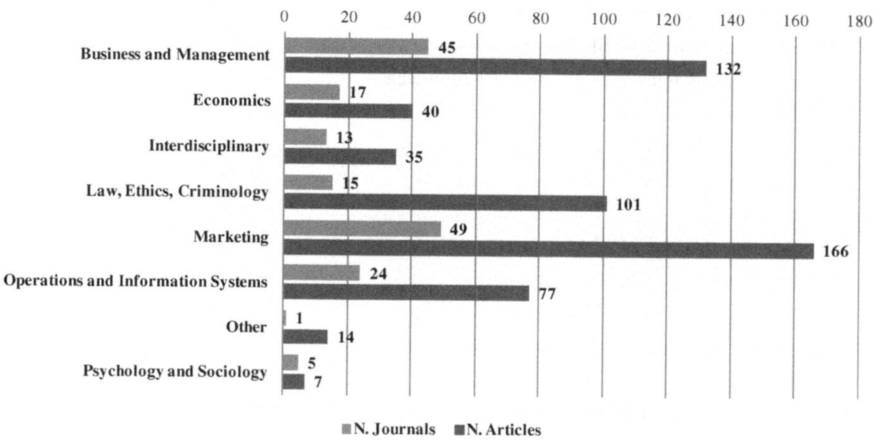

Fig. 3.1 Journals and articles per disciplinary area (*numbers*)

Table 3.2 Journal list, number of articles per journal (contributions order)

No.	Journal	Acronym	Total per journal
1	Journal of Business Ethics	JBE	57
2	Advances in Consumer Research	ACR	26
3	Business Horizons	BH	19
4	Communications of the ACM	CACM	18
5	The Journal of Consumer Marketing	JCM	14
6	n.a.	NA	14
7	Journal of Business Research	JBR	13
8	Review of Economic Research on Copyright Issues	RERCI	12
9	Intellectual Property and Technology Law Journal	IPTLJ	11
10	European Journal of Law and Economics	EJLE	10
11	Journal of Brand Management	JBM	9
12	Journal of Consumer Behavior	JCB	9
13	Journal of Internet Law	JIL	9
14	Journal of Management Information Systems	JMIS	8
15	Applied Economics Letters	AEL	7
16	Information & Management	I&M	7
17	Journal of Fashion Marketing and Management	JFMM	7
18	Journal of Marketing	JoM	7
19	Journal of Product & Brand Management	JP&BM	7
20	Management Science	MS	7
21	The China Business Review	CBR	6
22	International Journal of Marketing Studies	IJMS	6
23	Journal of Public Policy & Marketing	JPP&M	6
24	Marketing Intelligence & Planning	MI&P	6
25	The Columbia Journal of World Business	CJWB	5
26	European Journal of Marketing	EJM	5
27	International Journal of Electronic Commerce	IJEC	5
28	Information Systems Research	ISR	5
29	Journal of International Consumer Marketing	JICM	5
30	The Journal of World Intellectual Property	JWIP	5
31	Technovation	TECH	5
32	Asia Pacific Journal of Marketing and Logistics	APJML	4
33	The Journal of Industrial Economics	JIE	4
34	Journal of Marketing Management	JMM	4
35	Journal of Research in Interactive Marketing	JRIM	4
36	The Journal of Socio-Economics	JSE	4
37	The Multinational Business Review	MBR	4
38	Marketing Science	MktgS	4
39	Psychology & Marketing	P&M	4

(continued)

Table 3.2 (continued)

No.	Journal	Acronym	Total per journal
40	Business Ethics: A European Review	BEER	3
41	Business Strategy Review	BSR	3
42	Computers in Human Behavior	CHB	3
43	Computers in Industry	CI	3
44	Clothing and Textiles Research Journal	CTRJ	3
45	European Advances in Consumer Research	EACR	3
46	European Journal of Operational Research	EJOR	3
47	Economics Letters	EL	3
48	Harvard Business Review	HBR	3
49	Information & Communications Technology Law	I&CTL	3
50	International Journal of Industrial Organization	IJIO	3
51	International Journal of Management	IJM	3
52	Internet Research	IR	3
53	Journal of the Academy of Marketing Science	JAMS	3
54	Journal of Consumer Policy	JCP	3
55	Journal of Economic Behavior & Organization	JEB&O	3
56	Journal of International Marketing	JIMktg	3
57	Journal of Law and Economics	JLE	3
58	Journal of Business	JoB	3
59	Journal of World Business	JWB	3
60	Marketing Letters	MktgL	3
61	Virginia Law Review	VLR	3
62	Academy of Marketing Science Review	AMSR	2
63	Asia Pacific Journal of Management	APJM	2
64	Behavior & Information Technology	B&IT	2
65	Contributions to Economic Analysis & Policy	CEA&P	2
66	The Computer and Internet Lawyer	CIL	2
67	Consumption, Markets and Culture	CMC	2
68	European Economic Review	EER	2
69	Economic Inquiry	EI	2
70	European Management Journal	EMJ	2
71	International Journal of Information Management	IJIM	2
72	International Journal of Management Cases	IJMC	2
73	International Journal of Operations & Production Management	IJOPM	2
74	International Marketing Review	IMR	2
75	The Information Society: An International Journal	ISIJ	2
76	The Journal of Business Strategy	JBS	2
77	Journal of Consumer Affairs	JCA	2

(continued)

Table 3.2 (continued)

No.	Journal	Acronym	Total per journal
78	Journal of Economics	JE	2
79	Journal of Economics and Business	JE&B	2
80	Journal of Global Marketing	JGM	2
81	Journal of Internet Commerce	JIC	2
82	Journal of Information Systems	JIS	2
83	Journal of Marketing Theory and Practice	JMTP	2
84	Journal of Macromarketing	JoMM	2
85	Journal of Retailing	JoR	2
86	Journal of Retailing and Consumer Services	JRCS	2
87	Kyklos	KYK	2
88	Long Range Planning	LRP	2
89	Management Decision	MD	2
90	Management International Review	MIR	2
91	MIS Quarterly	MISQ	2
92	MIT Sloan Management Review	MITSMR	2
93	The Quarterly Journal of Economics	QJE	2
94	Qualitative Market Research: An International Journal	QMRIJ	2
95	R&D Management	R&DM	2
96	Topics in Economic Analysis and Policy	TEAP	2
97	Journal of Electronic Commerce Research	JECR	2
98	Advances in International Marketing	AIM	1
99	Academy of Information and Management Sciences Journal	AIMSJ	1
100	Asia Journal of Business Management	AJBM	1
101	Annals of Operations Research	AOR	1
102	Asia Pacific Business Review	APBR	1
103	Asia Pacific Journal of Business Administration	APJBA	1
104	Direct Marketing: An International Journal	DMIJ	1
105	European Business Review	EBR	1
106	Enterprise Information Systems	EIS	1
107	European Journal of Information Systems	EJIS	1
108	European Law Journal	ELJ	1
109	Financial Executive	FE	1
110	Global Trade and Customs Journal	GTCJ	1
111	International Journal of Business and Economics	IJBE	1
112	International Journal of Business and Social Science	IJBSS	1
113	International Journal of Business and Society	IJBS	1
114	International Journal of Consumer Studies	IJCS	1
115	International Journal of e-Education, e-Business, e-Management and e-Learning	IJeEeBeMeL	1

(continued)

Table 3.2 (continued)

No.	Journal	Acronym	Total per journal
116	International Journal of Production Research	IJPR	1
117	International Journal of Production Economics	IJPE	1
118	International Journal of Research in Marketing	IJRM	1
119	International Journal of Social Economics	IJSE	1
120	Industrial Marketing Management	IMM	1
121	International Review of Law and Economics	IRLE	1
122	The IUP Journal of Marketing Management	IUPJMM	1
123	The Journal of American Academy of Business	JAAB	1
124	The Journal of Applied Business Research	JABR	1
125	Journal of Applied Economics and Policy	JAEP	1
126	Journal of Asia-Pacific Business	JAPB	1
127	Journal of Advertising Research	JAR	1
128	Journal of Applied Social Psychology	JASP	1
129	Journal of Business & Economics Research	JB&ER	1
130	The Journal of Business and Industrial Marketing	JB&IM	1
131	Journal of Basic and Applied Scientific Research	JBASR	1
132	Journal of Behavioral and Experimental Economics	JBEE	1
133	Journal of Business Economics and Management	JBEM	1
134	Journal of Business and Retail Management Research	JBRMR	1
135	Journal of Brand Strategy	JBrS	1
136	Journal of Business and Technology Law	JBTL	1
137	Journal of Business Venturing	JBV	1
138	Journal of Economics & Management Strategy	JE&MS	1
139	Journal of East-West Business	JEWB	1
140	Journal of Global Information Technology Management	JGITM	1
141	Journal of International Business and Economics	JIB&E	1
142	Journal of International Business Ethics	JIBE	1
143	Journal of International Business Studies	JIBS	1
144	Journal of International Management	JIM	1
145	Journal of Legal, Ethical and Regulatory Issues	JLERI	1
146	Journal of Marketing and Management	JM&M	1
147	Journal of Marketing Research	JMR	1
148	Journal of Marketing Research and Case Studies	JMRCS	1
149	Journal of Nonprofit & Public Sector Marketing	JNPSM	1
150	Journal of Organizational Behavior Management	JOBM	1
151	Journal of Communication	JoC	1
152	Journal of Organization Computing and Electronic Commerce	JOCEC	1
153	Journal of Political Economy	JPE	1

(continued)

Table 3.2 (continued)

No.	Journal	Acronym	Total per journal
154	Journal of Proprietary Rights	JPR	1
155	Journal of Targeting, Measurement and Analysis for Marketing	JTMAM	1
156	Journal of World Trade	JWT	1
157	Latin American Advances in Consumer Research	LAACR	1
158	Media and Arts Law Review	MALR	1
159	Middle East Journal of Scientific Research	MEJSR	1
160	Managing Global Transitions	MGT	1
161	Managing Leisure	ML	1
162	The Marketing Review	MR	1
163	Psychological Science	PS	1
164	Psychology	Psych	1
165	Review of Business Research	RBR	1
166	Social Behavior and Personality	SBP	1
167	The Service Industries Journal	SIJ	1
168	Sociology	SOC	1
169	Theoretical and Applied Economics	TAE	1
TOTAL			**572**

Each article[5] was then analyzed using a spreadsheet to gather information regarding:

1. The year of publication;
2. The full name of the author(s);
3. The number of author(s);
4. The origin of the author(s) (country of university affiliation);
5. The journal where the article was published (acronym);
6. The type of study (either theoretical or empirical);
7. The number of citations (based upon the Google Scholar index)[6];
8. The distribution channel (physical/offline, digital/online, or both);
9. The industry/product category tested.

The volume moves now onto detailing all carried out analyses.

[5]The complete list of 572 articles examined is available from the Author upon request.

[6]Citations were continuously updated to take into account the new publications coming out. The last update was conducted as of September 5th 2015.

References

Furrer O, Thomas H, Goussevskaia A (2008) The structure and evolution of the strategic management field: a content analysis of 26 years of strategic management research. Int J Manage Rev 10(1):1–23

Lehnert K, Park Y-H, Singh N (2015) Research note and review of the empirical ethical decision-making literature: boundary conditions and extensions. J Bus Ethics 129(1):195–219

Srivastava SK (2007) Green supply-chain management: a state-of-the-art literature review. Int J Manage Rev 9(1):53–80

Webster J, Watson RT (2002) Analyzing the past to prepare for the future: writing a literature review. Manage Inf Syst Q 26(2):13–23

Zou S, Stan S (1998) The determinants of export performance: a review of the empirical literature between 1987 and 1997. Int Mark Rev 15(5):333–356

Chapter 4
Figures and Trends in the Academic Research on Counterfeiting and Piracy

Abstract The purpose of this chapter is to highlight the main figures and trends in the academic research on counterfeiting and piracy over the past 35 years. Through a descriptive analysis, the Author delves into the main typologies of studies (empirical vs. theoretical), methodologies (quantitative, qualitative and mixed), authors (productivity and countries-of-origin), citations (absolute vs. relative), products (counterfeit vs. pirated) and study contexts (online, offline, both). For the empirical papers, separate, dedicated attention is given to both quantitative and qualitative studies, in terms of data collection methods, conceptual frameworks, samples (typologies and countries-of-origin), and methodologies for analysis.

Keywords Trends · Typologies · Authorship · Industries · Study contexts

4.1 Results

As shown in Fig. 4.1, over the selected time period the number of scholarly contributions published on the topics in academic journals and magazines has sky-rocketed (see trend-line), with a peak of 52 articles in both 2006 and 2014. Since 1992, the number of contributions to the literature has risen every year with the exception of 1997, 2002, 2007, 2010, 2011 and 2013.[1]

4.1.1 Typologies

Among the articles analyzed, 196 (34.3 %) were purely theoretical while 376 (65.7 %) were empirical (Table 4.1; Fig. 4.2).

---

[1]We cannot account the total number of contributions of 2015 as a decrease since the year is not yet over.

L. Cesareo, *Counterfeiting and Piracy*,
SpringerBriefs in Business, DOI 10.1007/978-3-319-25357-2_4

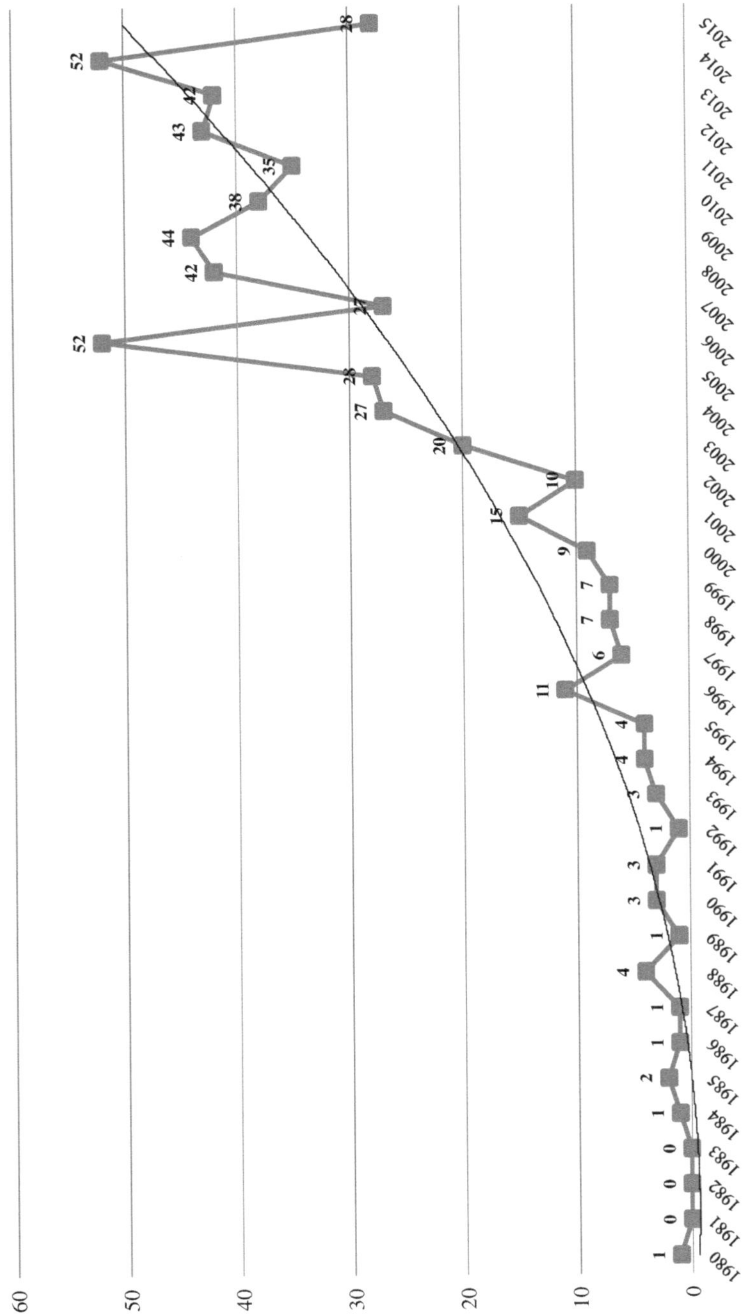

Fig. 4.1 Number of scholarly articles on counterfeiting/piracy per year (1980–2015) (2015 figure updated as of September)

Table 4.1 Number of theoretical and empirical papers per year

Year	1980	1984	1985	1986	1987	1988	1989	1990	1991	1992	1993	1994	1995	1996	1997	1998	1999
Theoretical	1	0	1	1	1	4	0	0	2	0	1	2	1	7	4	2	2
Empirical	0	1	1	0	0	0	1	3	1	1	2	2	3	4	2	5	5
Total	**1**	**1**	**2**	**1**	**1**	**4**	**1**	**3**	**3**	**1**	**3**	**4**	**4**	**11**	**6**	**7**	**7**
Year	2000	2001	2002	2003	2004	2005	2006	2007	2008	2009	2010	2011	2012	2013	2014	2015	Total (%)
Theoretical	4	5	5	6	11	12	23	12	15	15	8	8	8	14	14	7	**196 (34.3 %)**
Empirical	5	10	5	14	16	16	29	15	27	29	30	27	35	28	38	21	**376 (65.7 %)**
Total	**9**	**15**	**10**	**20**	**27**	**28**	**52**	**27**	**42**	**44**	**38**	**35**	**43**	**42**	**52**	**28**	**572 (100 %)**

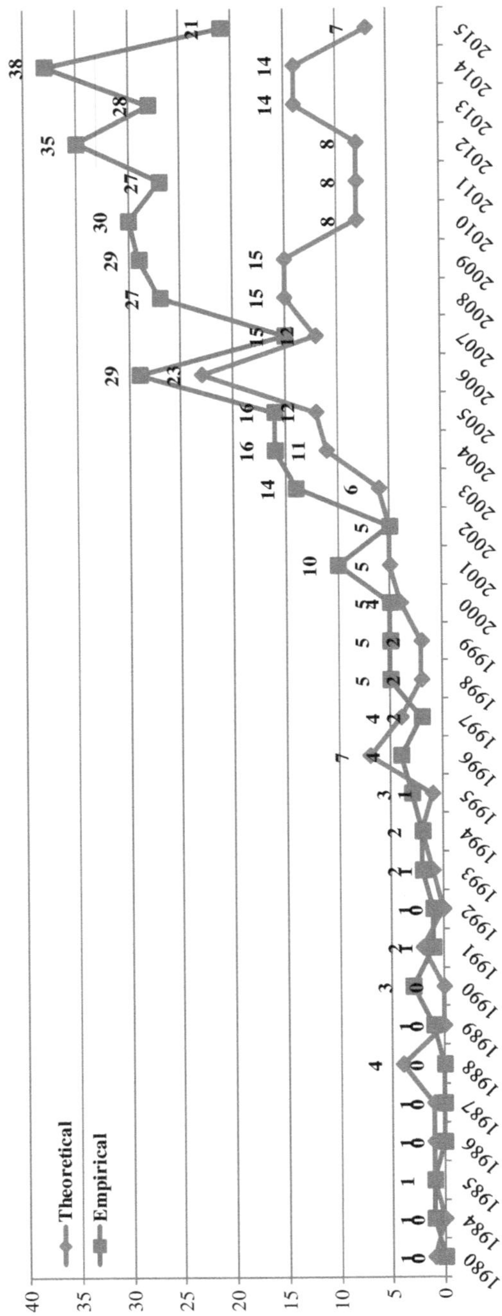

Fig. 4.2 Number of theoretical and empirical scholarly articles on counterfeiting/piracy per year (1980–2015)

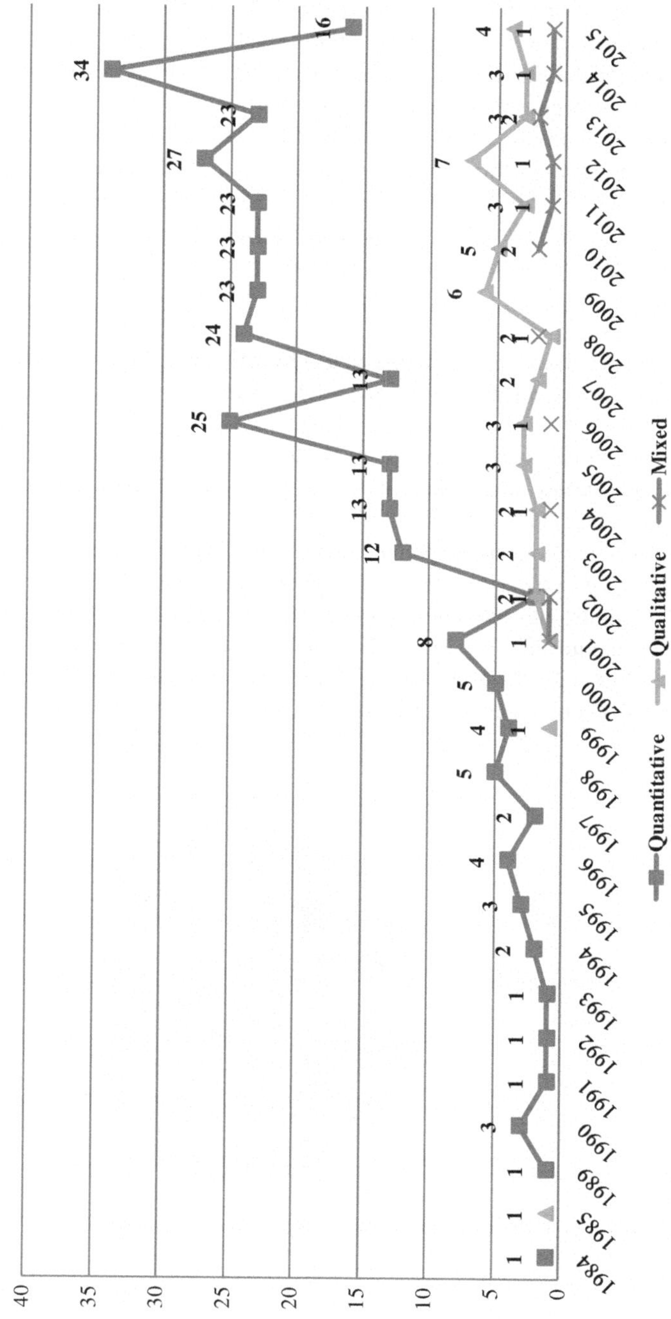

Fig. 4.3 Empirical papers by methodology (quantitative, qualitative, mixed) over time (*numbers*)

Empirical contributions have always surpassed theoretical contributions, with few exceptions towards the beginning of research on the phenomena (1980, 1986, 1987, 1988, 1991, 1996, 1997) and a tie in 1985 (1 theoretical and 1 empirical) and 2002 (5 theoretical and 5 empirical). In the past few years, the gap between empirical papers and theoretical papers has increased dramatically, with the greatest distance in 2013 (35 empirical vs. 8 theoretical articles).

Among the 376 empirical contributions, the majority (312 articles, 83.0 %) employed quantitative methodologies, 49 articles (13.0 %) employed qualitative methodologies while only 15 articles (4.0 %) had mixed methodologies (both quantitative and qualitative). The gap between quantitative methodologies and the others is even more evident when analyzed over time (Fig. 4.3).

4.1.1.1 A Deeper Look at the Empirical Quantitative Papers: Data Collection, Conceptual Frameworks, Samples and Analyses

Among the empirical quantitative papers, the most employed data collection method was the survey (80.8 %), followed by secondary data (industry reports, financial reports, etc.) (18.6 %) (Fig. 4.4).

Different were the conceptual frameworks tested. While many contributions did not make reference to a specific theory (91 papers), the ones that did mostly tested simple and complex attitude-intention models, referring back to the Theory of Reasoned Action and the Theory of Planned Behavior (Fishbein and Ajzen 1975; Ajzen 1991) (28.8 %), ethical and moral decision-making models (Kohlberg 1971; Hunt and Vitell 1986; Jones 1991; Rest 1994, etc.) (23.5 %) (Fig. 4.5).

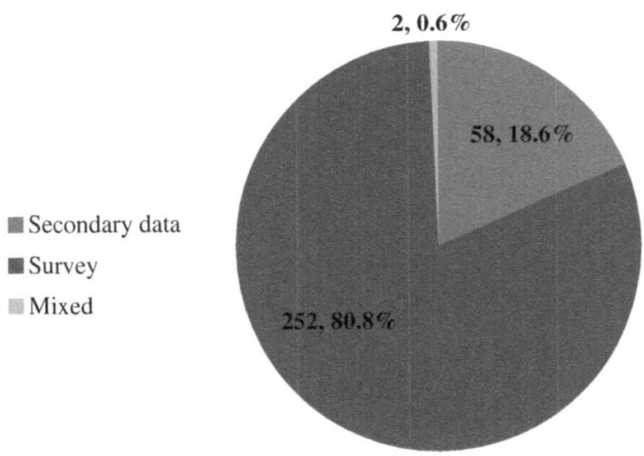

Fig. 4.4 Data collection methods in quantitative research (*no of articles, %*)

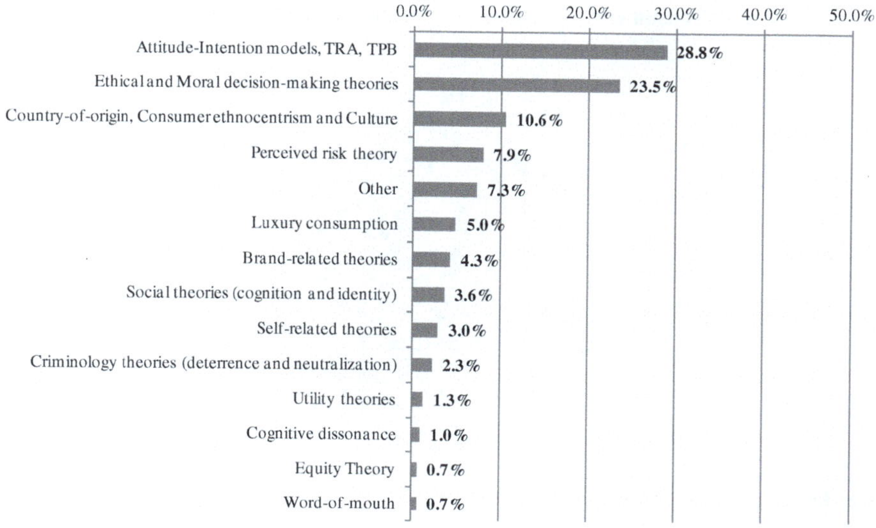

Fig. 4.5 Theories and conceptual frameworks tested quantitatively (%)

Among the studies that employed surveys as the data collection instrument (252 articles), it is interesting to highlight how most samples comprised consumers (226 articles, 89.68 %), 15 articles (5.95 %) comprised managers and manufacturers, while the remaining 11 articles (4.37 %) had mixed samples (Fig. 4.6).

Further delving into the consumer samples, in order to further understand who has been mainly targeted for studies on both counterfeiting and piracy, a deeper analysis unravels how 46.9 % of quantitative papers employing surveys have sampled adult (non-student) consumers while the majority (53.1 %) has sampled students at either university level (50.4 %), graduate level (1.3 %) or high school level (1.3 %) (Fig. 4.7).

Overall, consumer samples were mostly from a single country (196, 86.7 %), while few tested either two different countries (12, 5.3 %) or four or more countries (11, 4.8 %); only seven papers did not specify the consumers' country-of-origin or employed an online sample (7, 3.1 %). Consumer mostly came from the United States (3, 4.4 %), followed by China (8.6 %), the United Kingdom (7.4 %), Hong Kong (6.1 %) and Taiwan (6.1 %) (Fig. 4.8).

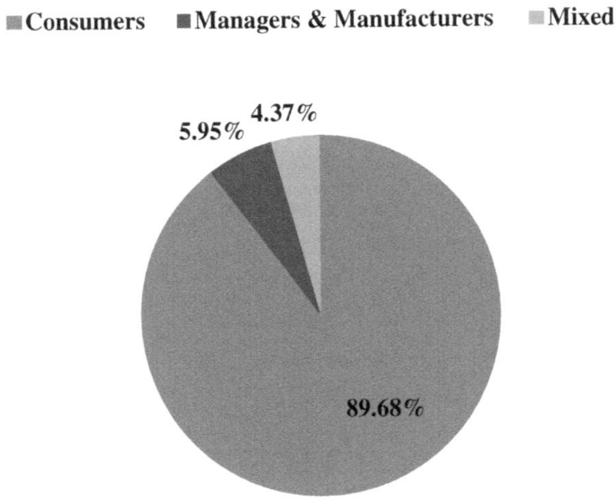

Fig. 4.6 Quantitative survey samples categories (%)

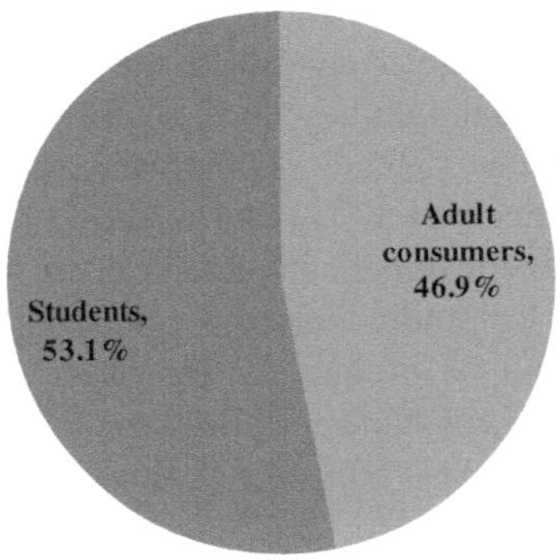

Fig. 4.7 Quantitative papers consumer sample typologies—adults (non-student) versus students (%)

In terms of methodologies employed to analyze the quantitative data, the most employed method was regression (105 papers, 33.1 %) followed by mixed methodologies (for example ANOVA and F-tests, factor analysis and path analysis, T-tests and regression, etc.—75 papers, 24.0 %) and path analyses or structural equations modeling (SEM) (59 articles, 18.9 %) (Figs. 4.9 and 4.10).

Among the papers that used regression, many did not further specify what kind of regression was employed (23.9 %); the ones that did mostly used multiple (17.0 %), followed by ordinary least squares (OLS) (12.6 %), logistic (11.9 %), linear (8.1 %), stepwise (7.4 %) and hierarchical (5.2 %) (Fig. 4.11).

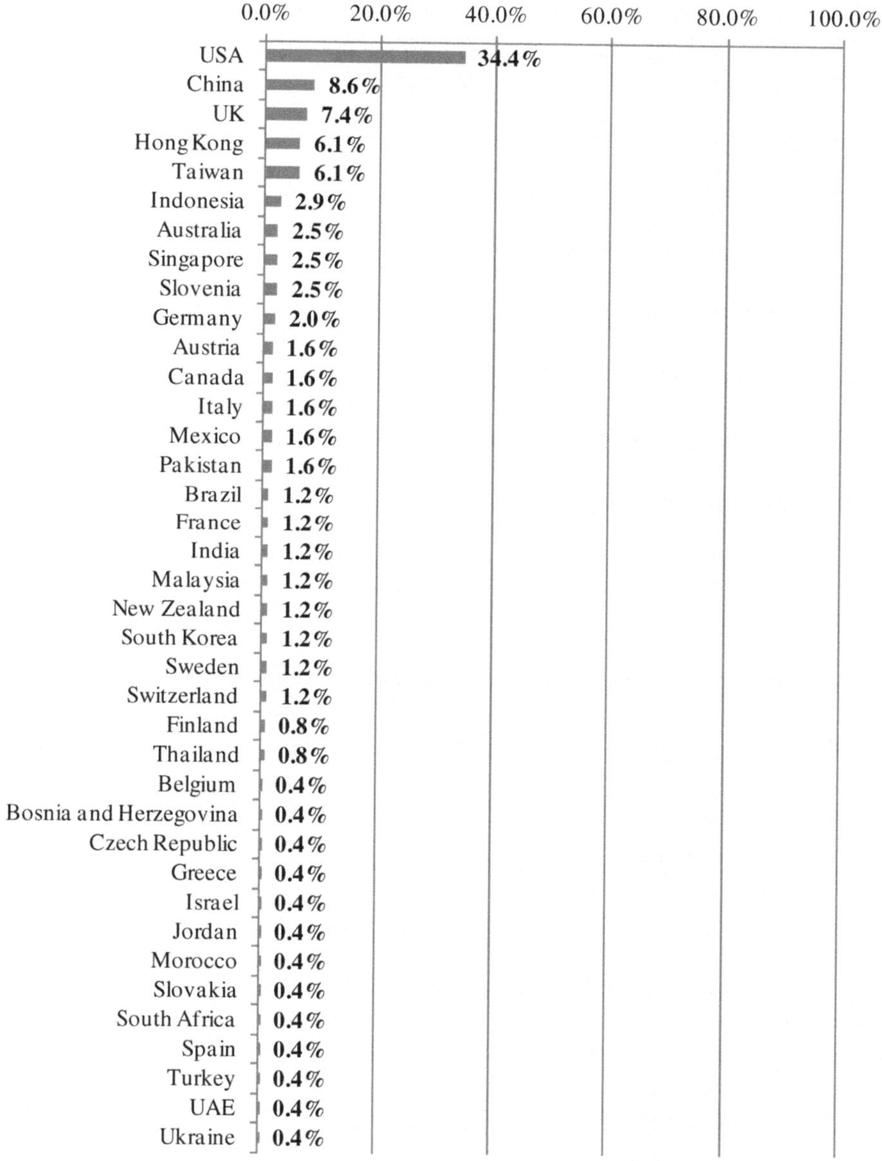

Fig. 4.8 Quantitative consumer samples (adults and students)—countries of origin (%)

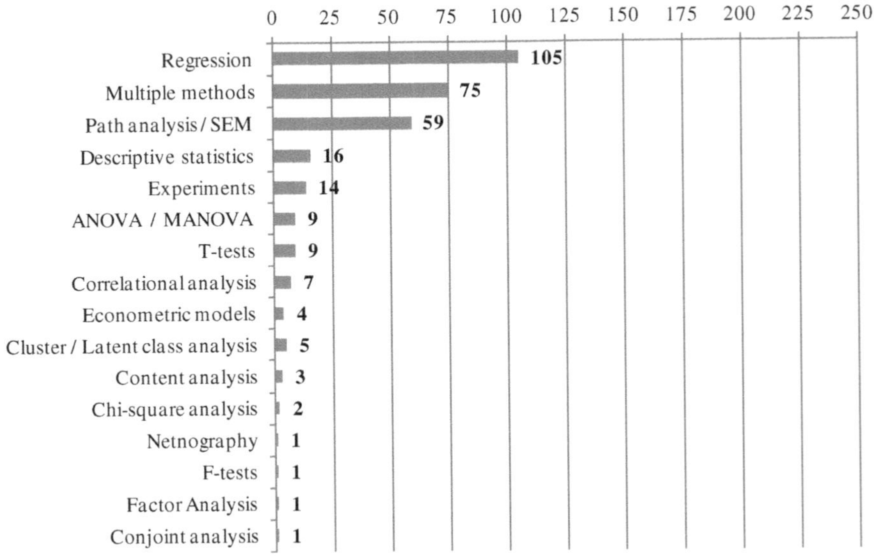

Fig. 4.9 Quantitative methodologies for analyses (*numbers*)

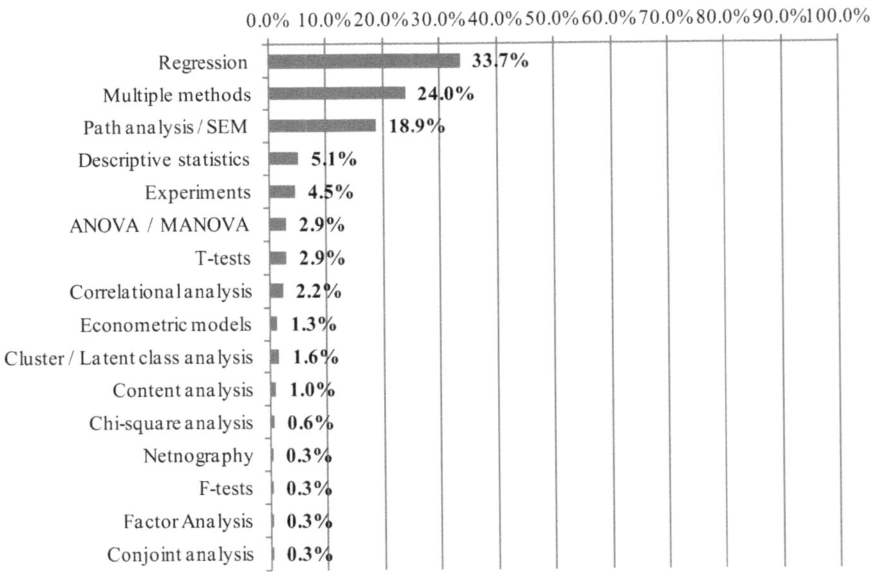

Fig. 4.10 Quantitative methodologies for analyses (%)

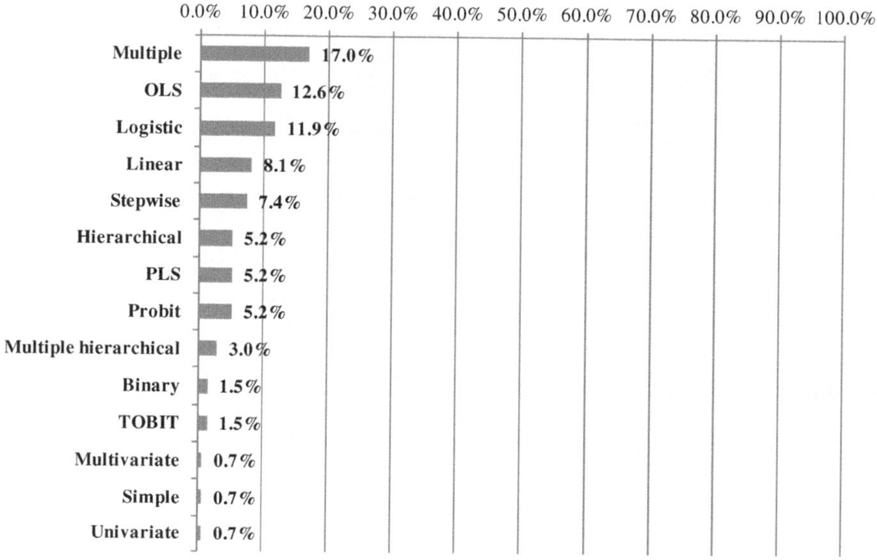

Fig. 4.11 Regression analyses (%)

4.1.1.2 A Deeper Look at the Empirical Qualitative Papers: Data Collection, Conceptual Frameworks, Samples and Analyses

Among the qualitative papers the most employed data collection method was in-depth interviews (31 articles, 63.3 %), followed by mixed methods (8 articles, 16.3 %) and focus groups (4 articles, 8.2 %) (Fig. 4.12).

Among the qualitative studies that employed in-depth interviews, focus groups and mixed methods (43 articles), it is interesting to highlight how most samples comprised consumers (23 articles, 53.5 %), 18 articles (41.95 %) comprised managers, companies and professionals, while the remaining 2 articles (4.7 %) involved governmental and legal entities (Fig. 4.13).

Fig. 4.12 Data collection methods in qualitative research (*no of articles, %*)

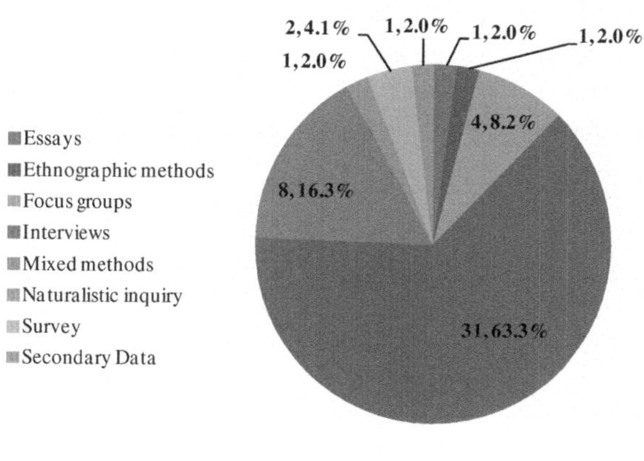

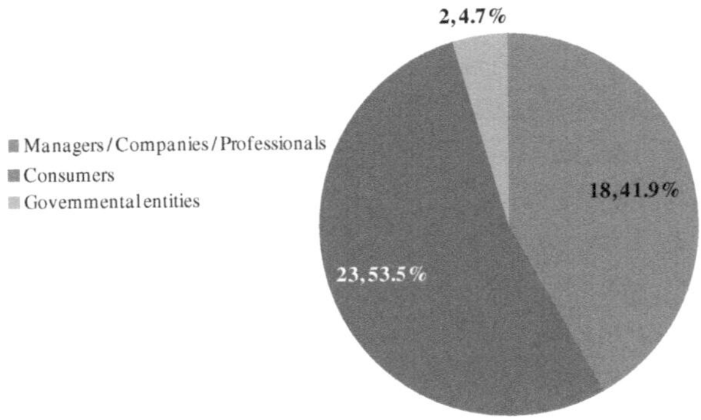

Fig. 4.13 Qualitative in-depth interview, focus groups and mixed methods samples categories (*no of articles*, *%*)

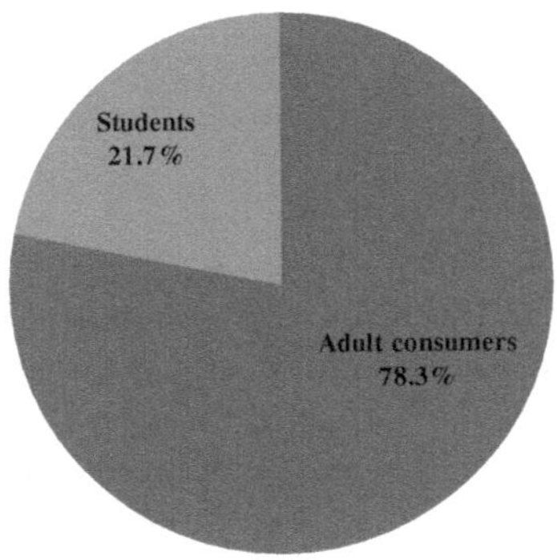

Fig. 4.14 Qualitative papers consumer sample typologies—adults (non-students) versus students (%)

Further delving into the consumer samples, the majority were adults (non-students) (78.3 %), while the remaining 21.7 % were students (Fig. 4.14).

Overall, consumer samples were mostly from a single country (17, 77.3 %), while only two contributions tested two different countries (2, 9.1 %) and a few articles included eight or more countries (3, 13.6 %). Consumers mainly came from Australia, China and India (10.3 % each), and from Austria, Germany, Mexico, Sweden and the USA (6.9 % each) (Fig. 4.15).

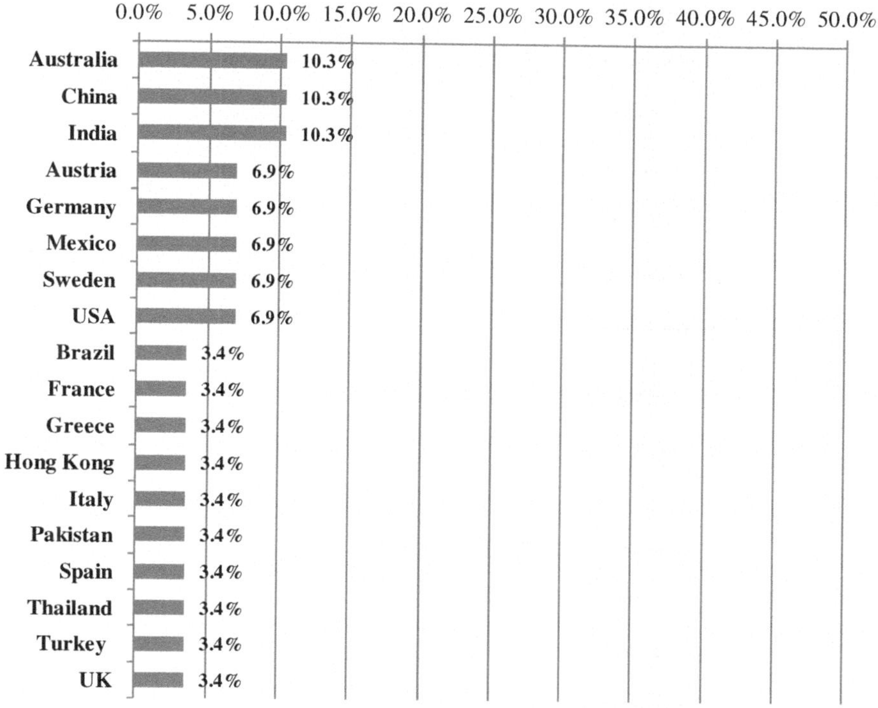

Fig. 4.15 Qualitative consumer samples (adults and students)—countries of origin (%)

In terms of methodologies employed to analyze the qualitative data, the most employed was content analysis (28 papers, 57.1 %) followed by and case study/ies (11 articles, 22.4 %) and descriptive analysis (7 papers, 14.3 %) (Figs. 4.16 and 4.17).

Among the papers that used content analysis, while half did not further specify what kind of analysis was employed, the ones that did mostly used thematic (30.8 %), followed by interpretative (15.4 %) and grounded theory (3.8 %) (Fig. 4.18).

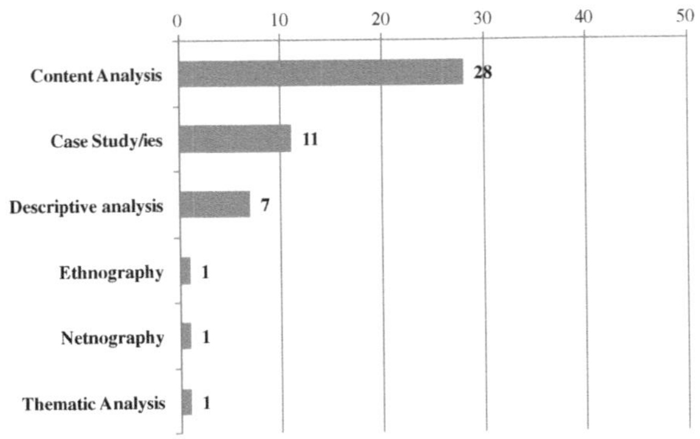

Fig. 4.16 Qualitative methodologies for analyses (*numbers*)

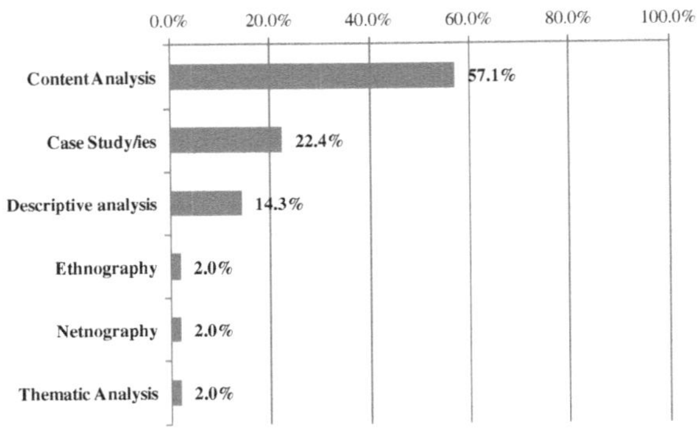

Fig. 4.17 Qualitative methodologies for analyses (%)

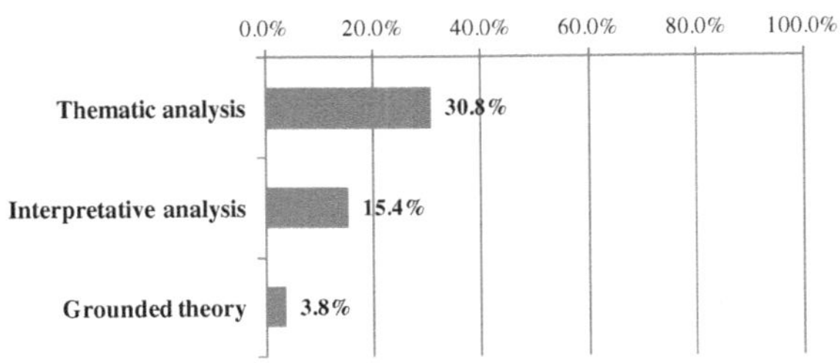

Fig. 4.18 Content analyses (%)

4.2 Authorship and Countries-of-Origin

In terms of Authorship, a total of 1254 authors (of which 924 *unique* authors) wrote the 572 articles, with an average of 2.19 authors per paper. The number of authors per article varied between one and seven: 144 articles (11.5 %) had only 1 author, 236 articles (18.8 %) had 2 authors, 141 articles (11.2 %) had 3 authors, 44 articles (3.5 %) had 4 authors, 5 articles (0.4 %) had 5 authors and 2 articles had 7 authors (0.2 %).

The most productive authors on counterfeiting and piracy are summarized in Table 4.2, while details for the authors who have written 5 or more articles each are provided below.

- **14 articles**: *Peggy E. Chaudhry*, of Villanova School of Business, Villanova University, USA, is the most productive author of all time. She has authored a total of 14 articles, of which 2 as a single author and 12 in co-authorship.
- **11 articles**: *Ian Phau*, Curtin University of Technology, Australia.
- **9 articles**: *Deli Yang*, Bradford University School of Management, UK.
- **8 articles**: *Ram D. Gopal*, University of Connecticut School of Business, USA.
- **7 articles**: *Elfriede Penz* and *Barbara Stoettinger*, Institute for International Marketing Management, Vienna University of Economics and Business, Austria; *Stephen A. Stumpf*, Villanova School of Business, Villanova University, USA.
- **6 articles**: *Xian Bian*, Business School, University of Nottingham, UK; *Alexander Nill*, Lee Business School, University of Nevada, USA; *G. Lawrence Sanders*, School of Management, State University of New York at Buffalo, USA; *Clifford J. Shultz*, II, Quinlan School of Business, Loyola University, USA.
- **5 articles**: *Timothy P. Cronan*, University of Arkansas, USA; *Gilles Grolleau*, LAMETA, France; *Mahmut Sonmez*, Loughborough University Business School, UK; *Alan Zimmerman*, College of Staten Island, the City University of New York, USA.

In terms of country-of-origin,[2] authors originated from 49 different countries across the five continents. Most of the authors lived in the United States (403, 43.68 %), followed by the United Kingdom (67, 7.2 %) and Taiwan (53, 5.7 %) (Fig. 4.19). Analyzing the articles over time, it is evident how the greatest number of contributions consistently comes from authors is the Americas, followed by European authors and Asian authors. Contributions of authors from both Africa and Oceania have only started with the turn of the 21st century (Fig. 4.20).

---

[2]The country-of-origin of each author was assessed based on the University affiliation at the time of article publication. If the affiliation changed between article publications, the latest affiliation was taken into account.

Table 4.2 The most productive authors (in terms of numbers of articles authored)

No. of articles authored	No. of authors	Author(s)
14 articles	1	Chaudhry, P.E.
11 articles	1	Phau, I.
9 articles	1	Yang, D.
8 articles	1	Gopal, R.D.
7 articles	3	Penz, E.; Stoettinger, B.; Stumpf, S.A.
6 articles	4	Bian, X.; Nill, A.; Sanders, G.L.; Shultz, C.J. II
5 articles	4	Cronan, T.P.; Grolleau, G.; Sonmez, M.; Zimmerman, A.
4 articles	21	Bhattacharjee, S.; Chan, R.Y.K.; Cordell, V.V.; Danaher, B.; El Harbi, S.; Fryxell, G.E.; Harvey, M.G.; Harvey, P.J.; Kim, J.E.; Koklic, M.K.; Kopp, S.W.; Moores, T.T.; Prendergast, G.; Qian, Y.; Smith, M.D.; Teah, M.; Telang, R.; Tjiptono, F.; Vida, I.; Walls, W.D.; Zaichkowsky, J.L.
3 articles	20	Andrés, A.R.; Bekir, I.; Crittenden, W.F.; Goode, M.M.H.; Khouja, M.; Langenderfer, J.; Lau, E.K.W.; Lee, S.H.; Mahajan, V.; Moutinho, L.; Perez, M.E.; Png, I.P.L.; Robertson, C.J.; Samuelson, P.; Sharma, P.; Suter, T.A.; Waelbroeck, P.; Waldfogel, J.; Yao, J.-T.; Yoo, B.
2 articles	125	Allred, A.T.; Al-Rafee, S.; Amaral, N.; Anwar Mir, I.; Ariely, D.; Arli, D.; Asongu, S.A.; Balkin, D.B.; Banerjee, D.S.; Beckenbauer, A.; Berman, B.; Bloch, P.H.; Bosworth, D.; Bristol, T.; Buff, C.L.; Bush, R.F.; Cesareo, L.; Chakraborty, G.; Chellappa, R.K.; Chen, Y.-C.; Cheng, H.K.; Cheung, W.-L.; Chuen, L.H.; Clark, D.; Cockrill, A.; Commuri, S.; Crittenden, V.; Cuadrado-Garcia, M.; d'Astous, A.; De Castro, J.O.; de Montoro-Pons, J.D.; Depken, C.A. II; Devinney, T. M.; Dix, S.; Domon, K.; Doss, F.; Easley, R.F.; Eckhardt, G. M.; Eining, M.M.; Eisend, M.; Farn, C.-K.; Ferreira, M.C.; Fleisch, E.; Furnham, A.; Gabrielli, V.; Gassman, O.; Giegner-Oneto, S.; Gentry, J.W.; Gillespie, K.; Gilley, K.M.; Gistri, G.; Goediertier, F.; Goode, S.; Gould, S.J.; Granzin, K. L.; Grappi, S.; Grossman, G.M.; Gupta, P.B.; Hennigs, N.; Higgins, G.E.; Huang, C.-Y.; Husted, B.W.; Jain, S.C.; Johnson, K.K.P.; Keupp, M.M.; Kim, H.K.; Klarmann, C.; Kocher, B.; Kwong, K.K.; Lertwachara, K.; Li, G.; Liao, C.-H.; Liebowitz, S.J.; Loken, B.; Lwin, M.; Maldonado, C.; Marcum, C.D.; Marsden, J.R.; Mitchell, V.-W.; Mittelstaedt, R.A.; Muller, B.; Nicholson, M.; Nunes, J.C.; Oberholzer-Gee, F.; Olsen, J.E.; Pace, S.; Park, J.; Peters, J.R.; Poddar, S.; Prasad, A.; Putrevu, S.; Quintanilla, C.; Rob, R.; Robinson, T.; Romani, S.; Ronkainen, I.A.; Schuchert-Guler, P.; Sequeira, M.; Shapiro, C.; Shivendu, S.; Simone, J.T.; Sims, R.R.; Sin, L.Y.M.; Sinha, R.K.; Smith, M.D.; Staake, T.; Strumpf, K.; Sudler, H.; Teegen, H.; Thiesse, F.; Tjiptono, F.; Thong, J.Y. L.; Ting, S.L.; Tsang, A.H.C.; Tse, A.C.B.; Veloutsou, C.; Wang, C.-C.; Wiedmann, K.-P.; Wooley, D.J.; Xiao, S.H.; Yao, J.-T.; Yang, Z.; Yau, O.H.M.; Zhang, H.; Zhu, H.

Fig. 4.19 Authors' country-of-origin (*descending order, numbers*)

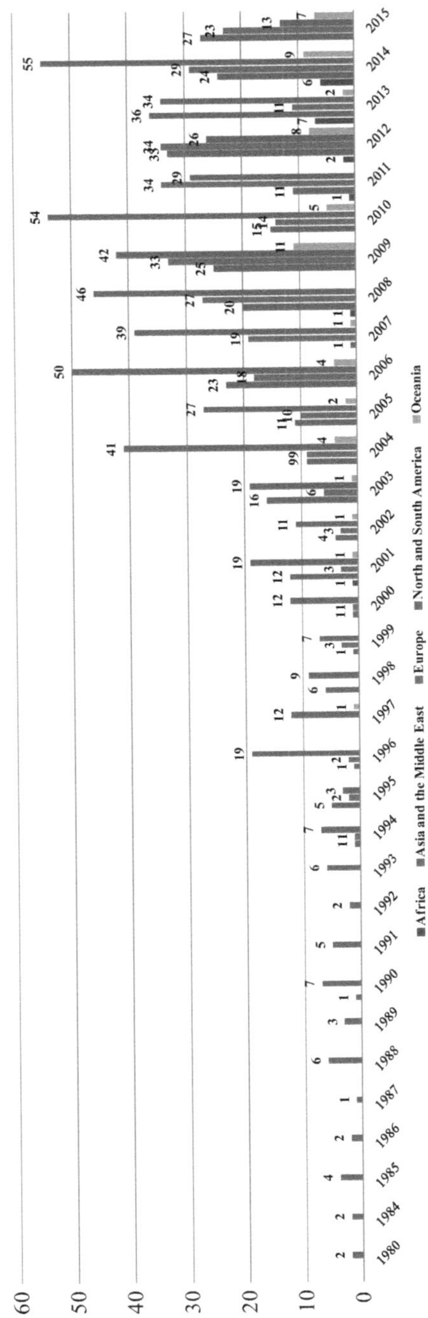

Fig. 4.20 Number of contributions based on authors' continent-of-origin over time

4.3 Citations

In terms of citations, both the absolute number (total number of citations per article) (Table 4.3) and the relative number (total number of citations in respect to the number of years the article has been published) (Table 4.4) need to be taken into account, since a paper published in an earlier period has a higher chance of having a larger number of citations than a paper published in a later period.[3]

Table 4.3 Top 10 most cited articles in absolute terms

Rank	Year	Title	Author(s)	Journal acronym	Citations
1	2007	The effect of file sharing on record sales: an empirical analysis	Oberholzer-Gee, F.; Strumpf, K.	JPE	887
2	1991	Software piracy: an analysis of protection strategies	Conner, K.R.; Rumelt, R.P.	MS	656
3	1998	Predicting unethical behavior: a comparison of the theory of reasoned action and the theory of planned behavior	Chang, M.K.	JBE	599
4	1994	The welfare implications of unauthorized reproduction of intellectual property in the presence of demand network externalities	Takeyama, L.N.	JIE	442
5	2006	Piracy on the high C'S: music downloading, sales displacement, and social welfare in a sample of college students	Rob, R.; Waldfogel, J.	JLE	421
6	2004	The composition of foreign direct investment and protection of intellectual property rights: evidence from transition economies	Javorcik, B.S.	EER	420
7	1988	Foreign counterfeiting of status goods	Grossman, G.M.; Shapiro, C.	QJE	400
8	2001	Spot the difference: consumer responses toward counterfeits	Ang, S.H.; Cheng, P.S.; Lim, E.A.C.; Tambyah, S.K.	JCM	396
9	2000	Do counterfeits devalue the ownership of luxury brands?	Nia, A.; Zaichkowsky, J.L.	JP & BM	395
10	2006	The piracy paradox: innovation and intellectual property in fashion design	Raustiala, K; Sprigman, C.	VLR	391

[3]Citations were updated from Google Scholar as of September 5th 2015.

In absolute terms, the most cited article of all time is "The Effect of File Sharing on Record Sales: An Empirical Analysis" published by Oberholzer-Gee and Strumpf, 2007 in the *Journal of Political Economy* with 887 citations. The article deals with the ongoing debate about the appropriate level of protection for intellectual property, mostly after the advent of the internet. The paper analyzes the effects of online file sharing on the legal sales of music through the employment of actual data on both downloads of music files and US record sales for a large number of albums. The authors discover how, in their data set, downloads have an effect on music sales that is statistically indistinguishable from zero and that therefore, according to their findings, file sharing is not the primary reason for the decline in music sales.

The second most-cited article of all time is "Software Piracy: An Analysis of Protection Strategies" authored by Reavis Conner and Rumelt 1991 published in *Management Science* with 656 citations. The paper develops an econometric model and suggests that in some circumstances, even with significant piracy, not protecting the software can be the best policy for the company since the positive externality, linked to the fact that piracy increases the total number of program users, raises profit firms and lowers selling prices.

The third most-cited article of all time is "Predicting Unethical Behavior: A Comparison of the Theory of Reasoned Action and the Theory of Planned Behavior" authored by Chang 1998 published in the *Journal of Business Ethics* with 599 citations, which compares the validity of the Theory of Reasoned Action (TRA) and the Theory of Planned Behavior (TPB) in predicting consumers' immoral behavior in relation to the illegal copying of software. The results of the structural equations modeling analysis reveal how the TPB is better than the TRA in predicting consumers' unethical behavior, since the added determinant of 'perceived behavioral control' is a better predictor of behavioral intention than attitude.

In relative terms though, i.e. dividing the absolute number of citations by the number of years the article has been published, while the first and most cited article remains the same one, all others change either in rank or in presence/absence. After Oberholzer-Gee and Strumpf's (2007) article (still the most cited, with 110.88 citations per year), the second most cited article is "Signaling Status with Luxury Goods: the Role of Brand Prominence" by Han et al. (2010) published in the *Journal of Marketing* with 63.20 citations per year. The article mainly deals with original luxury goods and creates a taxonomy of luxury goods consumers based upon wealth and need-for-status: Patricians, Parvenu, Proletarian and Poseurs. Among these four categories, those consumers who are high in need for status but cannot afford true luxury (*poseurs*) use loud counterfeits to emulate those they recognize to be wealthy.

The third most cited article is "Why do Consumers Buy Counterfeit Luxury Brands?" by Wilcox et al. (2009), in the *Journal of Marketing Research* with 48.67 citations per year. The article demonstrates that consumers prefer luxury counterfeits to original luxury products when their luxury brand attitudes serve a social-adjustive rather than a value-expressive function. Their moral beliefs about counterfeits, on the other hand, affect their counterfeit brand preferences only when their luxury brand attitudes serve a value-expressive function (Table 4.4).

Table 4.4 Top 10 most cited articles in relative terms (citations/year)

Rank	Year	Title	Author(s)	Journal acronym	Citations/Years
1	2007	The effect of file sharing on record sales: an empirical analysis	Oberholzer-Gee, F.; Strumpf, K.	JPE	110.88
2	2010	Signaling status with luxury goods: the role of brand prominence	Han, Y.J.; Nunes, J.C.; Drèze, X.	JoM	63.20
3	2009	Why do consumers buy counterfeit luxury brands?	Wilcox, K.; Kim, H.K.; Sen, S.	JMR	48.67
4	2006	Piracy on the high C'S: music downloading, sales displacement, and social welfare in a sample of college students	Rob, R.; Waldfogel, J.	JLE	46.78
5	2006	The piracy paradox: innovation and intellectual property in fashion design	Raustiala, K; Sprigman, C.	VLR	43.44
6	2006	File sharing: creative destruction or just plain destruction?	Liebowitz, S.J.	JLE	40.22
7	2004	The composition of foreign direct investment and protection of intellectual property rights: evidence from transition economies	Javorcik, B.S.	EER	38.18
8	1998	Predicting unethical behavior: a comparison of the theory of reasoned action and the theory of planned behavior	Chang, M.K.	JBE	35.12
9	2003	Software piracy in the workplace: a model and empirical test	Peace, A.G.; Galletta, D.F.; Thong, J.Y.L.	JMIS	30.50
10	2001	Spot the difference: consumer responses toward counterfeits	Ang, S.H.; Cheng, P.S.; Lim, E.A.C.; Tambyah, S.K.	JCM	28.29

4.4 Study Context

Counterfeit and pirated goods have always been available for purchase in traditional contexts through physical distribution channels, either *impromptu* vendors on street corner or organized flea markets and malls in different cities around the globe. The advent of the Internet has completely changed the distribution and the access to such products: peer-to-peer (P2P) networks, auction websites, copycat websites and search engines have tenfold the phenomena, making products available for purchase or free download 24 h a day, 7 days a week with a simple mouse-click. This shift has also been reflected in the academic literature: while in the earlier contributions authors focused solely on physical settings, which still today constitute key circulation channels for both counterfeiters and consumers worldwide, with the turn of the century researchers started analyzing the new digital setting, either by itself or in combination with the offline channels. As reflected in Fig. 4.21, the majority of works regards the traditional (offline) distribution channels (350 articles, 61.1 %), 124 articles (21.7 %) analyze the digital (online) distribution channel while 98 articles (17.1 %) analyze offline and online distribution channels jointly. Looking at the distribution channels over time (Fig. 4.22), it is evident how traditional channels have dominated in the past, while digital and joint distribution channel analyses have increased since the turn of the 21st century, with the gap reducing as of 2013.

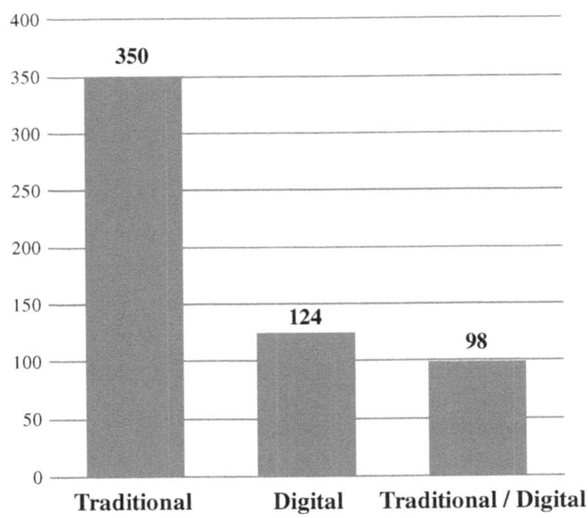

Fig. 4.21 Number of contributions per distribution channel (*overall*)

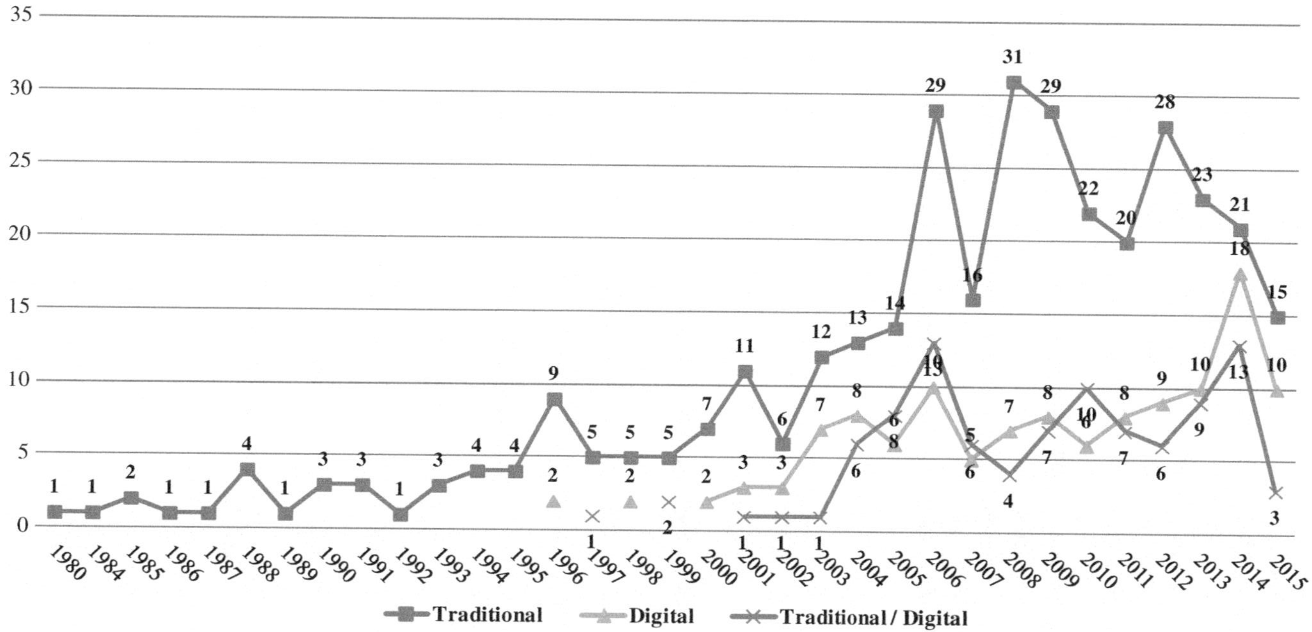

Fig. 4.22 Evolution of the studied distribution channels (traditional, digital, traditional/digital) over time (*numbers*)

4.5 Industries and Product Categories

As outlined in the Introduction to the volume, different are the industries and product categories hit by counterfeiting and piracy; it is therefore worth understanding which ones have been most studied by the academic literature. Out of the 572 articles analyzed, 162 articles did not make a direct reference to any specific industry, discussing counterfeit and/or pirated goods in general. Among the remaining 410 articles, it is very interesting to highlight how most have analyzed the software industry (92 studies, 22.4 %) and the music industry (91 studies, 22.2 %—in both physical CD format and online Mp3 format), followed by the overall media industries (movie, music, software, print, video games) (61 studies, 14.9 %—both offline and digital), the luxury goods industry (52 studies, 12.7 %—luxury apparel and accessories) and the fashion industry (apparel and accessories) (48 studies, 11.7 %) (Figs. 4.23 and 4.24).

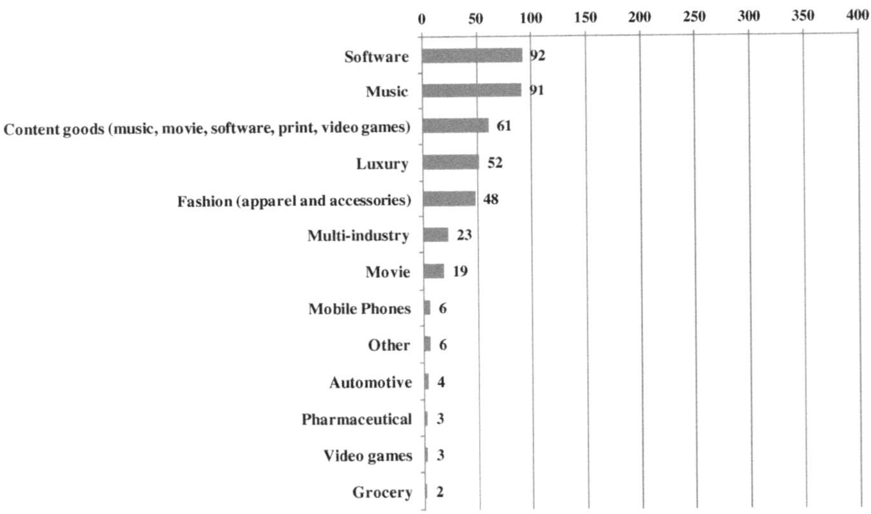

Fig. 4.23 Industries and product categories affected by counterfeiting/piracy most studied in the academic literature (*numbers*)

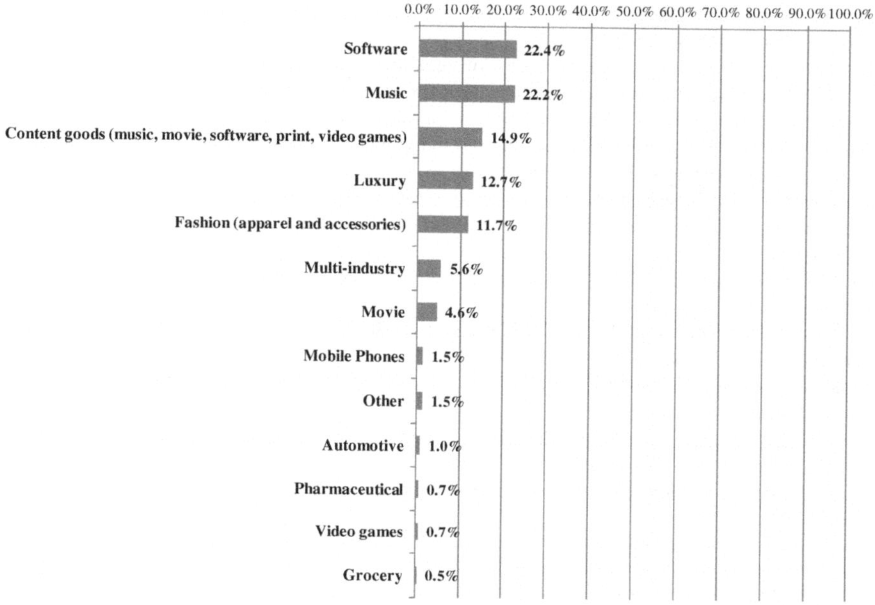

Fig. 4.24 Industries and product categories affected by counterfeiting/piracy most studied in the academic literature (%)

4.6 Conclusion

This chapter delved deeply and descriptively into the past 35 years of academic literature on counterfeiting and piracy, highlighting trends and figures in terms of typologies, methodologies, samples, methods of analyses, authorship, citations, product categories, industries and distribution channels. It is now important to delve into the same literature from a content, theoretical perspective. We turn to do so in the following chapter.

References

Ajzen I (1991) The theory of planned behavior. Organizational Behav Hum Decis Processes 50 (2):179–211

Ang SH, Cheng PS, Lim EA, Tambyah SK (2001) Spot the difference: consumer responses towards counterfeits. J Consum Mark 18(3):219–235

Chang MK (1998) Predicting unethical behavior: a comparison of the theory of reasoned action and the theory of planned behavior. J Bus Ethics 17(16):1825–1834

Fishbein M, Ajzen I (1975) Belief, attitude, intention and behavior: an introduction to theory and research. Addison-Wesley, MA

Grossman GM, Shapiro C (1988) Foreign counterfeiting of status goods. National Bureau of Economic Research, Cambridge

Han YJ, Nunes JC, Drèze X (2010) Signaling status with luxury goods: the role of brand prominence. J Mark 74(4):15–30
Hunt SD, Vitell S (1986) A general theory of marketing ethics. J Macromark 6(1):5–16
Javorcik BS (2004) The composition of foreign direct investment and protection of intellectual property rights: Evidence from transition economies. Eur Econ Rev 48(1):39–62
Jones TM (1991) Ethical decision making by individuals in organizations: an issue-contingent model. Acad Manag Rev 16(2):366–395
Kohlberg L (1971) Stages of moral development. Moral Educ:23–92.
Liebowitz SJ (2006) File sharing: creative destruction or just plain destruction?*. J Law Econ 49 (1):1–28
Nia A, Zaichkowsky JL (2000) Do counterfeits devalue the ownership of luxury brands? J Prod Brand Manag 9(7):485–497
Oberholzer-Gee F, Strumpf K (2007) The effect of file sharing on record sales: an empirical analysis. J Polit Econ 115(1):1–42
Peace AG, Galletta DF, Thong JY (2003) Software piracy in the workplace: a model and empirical test. J Manag Inf Syst 20(1):153–177
Raustiala K, Sprigman C (2006) The piracy paradox: innovation and intellectual property in fashion design. Va Law Rev:1687–1777.
Reavis Conner K, Rumelt RP (1991) Software piracy: an analysis of protection strategies. Manag Sci 37(2):125–139
Rest JR (1994) Background: theory and research. In: Moral development in the professions: psychology and applied ethics, pp 1–26.
Rob R, Waldfogel J (2006) Piracy on the high C's: music downloading, sales displacement, and social welfare in a sample of college students. J Law Econ 49:29–62
Takeyama LN (1994) The welfare implications of unauthorized reproduction of intellectual property in the presence of demand network externalities. J Ind Econ:155–166
Wilcox K, Kim HM, Sen S (2009) Why do consumers buy counterfeit luxury brands? J Mark Res 46(2):247–259

Chapter 5
Content Analysis and Categorization: Towards a Systematization of the Literature on Counterfeiting and Piracy

Abstract The purpose of this chapter is to provide the results of the content analysis of the 572 collected articles. After having read all the articles, and based upon the categorization scheme proposed by the most recent and general literature review (Staake et al. 2009), the Author classifies each article based upon its main themes, objectives and contributions into one (or more) of six categories. Among these, the demand-side analysis (DSI), which delves into consumer attitudes, intentions and behaviors towards illicit goods, is the absolute richest followed by the anti-counterfeiting/piracy strategies, tools and actions (ACSTA) employed by companies to fight against these instances.

Keywords Content analysis · Themes · Categorization · Consumer behavior · Anti-counterfeiting strategies · Tools and actions

The next step in the research was to analyze and categorize the articles according to their content. Counterfeiting and piracy have been addressed in the literature from different perspectives: demand-side, supply-side, economic, governmental, legal, strategic, etc.

Based on previous literature reviews on the topic (Staake et al. 2009), and after having read all the articles, six were the main thematic categories that emerged:

1. *General descriptions of the phenomena* (*GD*);
2. *International and national legal, political and economic frameworks on counterfeiting and piracy* (*IF*);
3. *Effects of counterfeiting/piracy* (*EoC*);
4. *Demand-side investigations* (*DSI*);
5. *Supply-side investigations* (*SSI*);
6. *Anti-counterfeiting/piracy strategies, tools and actions* (*ACSTA*).

In order to categorize the articles, a bibliographic note card was written to summarize the purpose, the methodology and the findings of each of the 572 articles. Examples of bibliographic note cards for both a theoretical and empirical paper can be found in Tables 5.1 and 5.2.

L. Cesareo, *Counterfeiting and Piracy*,
SpringerBriefs in Business, DOI 10.1007/978-3-319-25357-2_5

Table 5.1 Example of a bibliographical note card for a theoretical article

Author(s)	Juggessur, J.; Cohen, G.
Title	Is fashion promoting counterfeit brands?
Year	2009
Journal, volume, issue, pages	Journal of brand management, 16(5), 383–394
Country	Brunei, Brunei
Typology	Theoretical
Purpose	Analyze the demand side of high-fashion brands
Method, sample, analysis	–
Abstract	The aim of this conceptual paper is to address how the role of fashion and the public display of high fashion brands have contributed to the development of counterfeited brands. The fashion industry is a multimillion-pound industry, and many consumers use branded commodities as a way of creating identity. The consumption of high-fashion brands can hold social meaning, allowing consumers to express to others and themselves their individual and social characteristics through material possessions. High-fashion brands have instant global recognition, although the desire for these brands has opened up a market for counterfeited versions. This paper focuses on the demand side of high-fashion brands. In order to fully understand the context of fashion, a review of the abstract symbolic appeals aims to provide insight into the role of fashion and the antecedents of consumers opting for high-fashion brands and high-fashion counterfeit brands. It concludes with new insights into consumer behavior, and highlights managerial strategies for marketers of high-fashion brands
Main findings/contributions	The authors discuss the Veblen, snob, bandwagon effects plus the perfectionist and hedonic effect in both counterfeit and original fashion goods consumption
Category	GD, DSI, OCB
Channel/market	Traditional/offline

The Author categorized all the 572 articles herself, allowing for articles to fall (where required) under more than category. On the articles that created doubts as to their assignment, the Author asked two senior researchers, experts in the counterfeiting and piracy fields, to content analyze the articles and assign them separately to one (or more) of the six categories. If the majority of the researchers agreed upon the categorization, the article was directly assigned to the respective category/ies; otherwise, the researchers debated until a shared solution was found.

Among the 572 articles, 461 articles (80.6 %) were single category, 90 articles (15.7 %) were assigned to two categories, 20 (3.5 %) were assigned to three categories while only 1 article (0.2 %) was assigned to four categories (Table 5.3).

Table 5.2 Example of a bibliographical note card for an empirical article

Author(s)	Penz, E.; Stöttinger, B.
Title	Corporate image and product similarity—assessing major demand drivers for counterfeits in a multi-country study
Year	2008
Journal, volume, issue, pages	Psychology and marketing, 25(4), 352–381
Country	Austria, Austria
Typology	Empirical
Purpose	Study if corporate image and product attributes influence consumer attitudes and behavior towards counterfeit brands
Method, sample, analysis	Survey, 1846 consumers (1040 Austria, 213 Sweden, 211 Ukraine, 130 Slovakia, 128 US, 125 Mexico), ANOVA, Regression
Abstract	The demand for counterfeits has become a major headache for brand name manufacturers across the globe. This paper investigates two key demand drivers: (1) corporate image, in the form of evaluative and descriptive judgments of the original manufacturer and the counterfeiter, and (2) product attributes, split into physical, beneficial, and symbolic aspects, and their impact on consumers' intentions to buy fakes, based on the tripartite model of attitudes and by applying Peabody's concept of un-confounding evaluative and descriptive judgments (Peabody 1984; Peabody and Goldberg 1989; Saucier 1994; Saucier et al. 2001). In total, 1846 consumers were surveyed in six different countries: the United States, Austria, Mexico, Sweden, Slovakia, and the Ukraine. According to the results, corporate image and product characteristics show a strong impact on the consumers' intention to buy fakes. The relative importance of the concepts' sub-dimensions, however, differs substantially across the countries selected. With respect to the corporate image, respondents use mainly emotional responses to describe the image of original manufacturers and counterfeiters, and they clearly distinguish them based on image. Product-level comparisons revealed that looks, functionality, image, and physical appearance differed between originals and fakes across countries, whereas quality and durability of originals and fakes are perceived very similarly. The paper closes with managerial implications and avenues for future research
Main findings/contributions	Producers of originals are perceived more positively than counterfeiters; durability and quality of originals are perceived to be similar to those of counterfeits
Category	DSI, OCB, PrF, SoF, SiF
Channel/market	Traditional/Offline

Table 5.3 Overview of categories per article per year (*numbers*, %)

Category / year	1 Category	2 Categories	3 Categories	4 Categories	Total (Categories/year)
1980		1			1
1984	1				1
1985	1		1		2
1986	1				1
1987	1				1
1988	2		2		4
1989	1				1
1990	3				3
1991	3				3
1992		1			1
1993	2	1			3
1994	3	1			4
1995	4				4
1996	7	4			11
1997	6				6
1998	7				7
1999	6	1			7
2000	7	2			9
2001	12	2	1		15
2002	9		1		10
2003	16	4			20
2004	20	6	1		27
2005	20	7	1		28
2006	36	13	3		52
2007	18	6	3		27
2008	32	8	2		42
2009	36	8			44
2010	35	1	2		38
2011	27	6	2		35
2012	42	1			43
2013	35	5	1	1	42
2014	44	8			52
2015	24	4			28
Total	**461**	**90**	**20**	**1**	**572**
%	**80.6**	**15.7**	**3.5**	**0.2**	**100.0**

Table 5.4 Overview of articles per category per year (*numbers*, %)

Category Year	ACSTA	DSI	EoC	GD	IF	SSI	Total (categories)	Total (articles)
1980	1			1			2	1
1984			1				1	1
1985	1	1		1		1	4	2
1986						1	1	1
1987	1						1	1
1988	1	2	2	2	1		8	4
1989	1						1	1
1990		2	1				3	3
1991		1	1		1		3	3
1992	1					1	2	1
1993	1	1			1	1	4	3
1994		2	2	1			5	4
1995		2	1	1			4	4
1996	5	4		2	3	1	15	11
1997		2		3	1		6	6
1998	1	5			1		7	7
1999	2	2	1	2	1		8	7
2000	2	4	2		2	1	11	9
2001	2	10	1	3	3		19	15
2002	5	2		1	3	1	12	10
2003	2	11	4			7	24	20
2004	8	13	2	5	2	5	35	27
2005	5	12	5	3	7	5	37	28
2006	8	26	10	9	8	10	71	52
2007	4	14	7	5	4	5	39	27
2008	4	26	9	5	5	5	54	42
2009	7	23	3	10	6	3	50	44
2010	3	25	4	4	3	4	42	38
2011	2	26	3	3	4	7	45	35
2012	3	32	4	3	1	1	44	43
2013	10	28	4	4	3	3	52	42
2014	3	30	13	2	5	7	27	52
2015	4	18	4	0	2	4	32	28
Total	**87**	**324**	**84**	**70**	**67**	**73**	**705**	**572**
%	**12.3**	**46.0**	**11.9**	**9.9**	**9.5**	**10.4**	**100**	**100.0**

Taking the possible multiple categories of each paper into account,[1] the most numerous category was—by far—the demand-side investigations (46.0 %), followed by the anti-counterfeiting strategies, tools and actions (12.3 %), the effects of counterfeiting (11.9 %), the supply-side investigations (10.4 %), the general descriptions (9.9 %), and finally the international and national frameworks (9.5 %). A summary of the articles per category, per year is given in Table 5.4. The Author then turns to describe each category in detail.

5.1 General Descriptions of the Phenomena

Papers in this category tend to describe the importance of counterfeiting and piracy for both public and private groups, while highlighting the relevance to both theory and practice. Earlier contributions defined the issues, the scopes of the phenomena and the legal and economic changes that would be necessary to govern them, in a forward-looking perspective (Grossman and Shapiro 1988; Nill and Shultz II 1996; Thurow 1997); more recent contributions focused on the evolution of the phenomena over time, adopting more of a retrospective perspective (Chaudhry et al. 2009; Nill and Shultz II 2009; Novos and Waldman 2013). With the emergence of the knowledge economy and the advent of new digital technologies, for example, the whole concept of Intellectual Property enforcement needs to be revised and modernized.

5.2 International and National Legal, Political and Economic Frameworks on Counterfeiting and Piracy

Previous literature describing the national and an international legal framework governing counterfeiting and piracy worldwide, has emphasized the difficulties governmental entities face in normative enforcement, mostly in the digital setting. On an international level, articles have discussed, for example, the World Trade Organization's (WTO) TRIPs agreement (Trade-Related aspects on Intellectual Property rights) and the Anti-Counterfeiting Trade Agreement (ACTA), and the difficulties in international IPRs enforcement (linked, for example, to the scarce, yet necessary, national government cooperation in actual enforcement on the territory) (Bender 2006; Jain 1996; Roy 2007; Jandhyala 2015). On a national level, previous literature has focused on the Digital Millennium Copyright Act (DMCA) and other laws governing IPRs in the United States and in Europe or national Chinese law governing IP protection and enforcement (Lunney 2001; Yang and Clarke 2005;

[1]Since a paper could fall under more than one category, the total number of articles/category is greater than the total number of articles (705 vs. 572).

Chaudhry 2006; Ferrante 2015). More recently, a greater emphasis has been placed upon the difficulties in ruling against counterfeiting and piracy online (Kopp and Suter 2000; Chaudhry et al. 2011a; Scott 2013; Payne 2014), with often references to real life cases (Louis Vuitton vs. eBay in France, Van Eecke and Truyens 2008).

5.3 Effects of Counterfeiting/Piracy

Articles studying the effects of counterfeiting and piracy on legitimate companies have underlined different aspects. A first group of studies has developed econometric models to understand whether counterfeiting and piracy generate solely negative effects on companies, consumers, countries and overall societal welfare, or if, under some circumstances (such as network effects, sampling effects, vertical differentiation, different degrees of contractual and IP enforcement, presence of barriers of entry and different pricing levels) they should be partially tolerated since they can increase overall profits (i.e. Peitz and Waelbroeck 2006; Takeyama 1994; Chen and Png 2003; De Castro et al. 2007; Givon et al. 1995; Grassi 2014; Qian 2014b; Ma et al. 2014). A second group of studies has delved into the effects of file-sharing technologies and peer-to-peer networks on physical sales of content goods, employing mostly secondary data and regression analyses (i.e. Zentner 2005; Liebowitz 2006; Hennig-Thurau et al. 2007; Oberholzer-Gee and Strumpf 2010; Smith and Telang 2009; Das et al. 2014; Koh et al. 2014). Finally, a third group of studies has analyzed the impact of counterfeiting on both consumer perceptions of original brands and companies' efforts in brand management (Wilke and Zaichkowsky 1999; Nia and Zaichkowsky 2000; Qian 2014a).

5.4 Demand-Side Investigations

The richest category in the counterfeiting and piracy literature, contrary to recurring claims, is the one focusing on consumer behavior, in terms of determinants of attitude towards counterfeiting and piracy, and consumer intentions. Studies have addressed the issue of consumer complicity and the demand for illicit goods (both counterfeit and pirated) from both theoretical and empirical perspectives, adopting, in the latter, mostly quantitative approaches.

The most tested theories and conceptual models have been simple and complex attitude-intention models referring back to the Theory of Reasoned Action (TRA) and the Theory of Planned Behavior (TPB) (Fishbein and Ajzen 1975; Ajzen 1991), followed by ethical and moral decision-making models (Hunt and Vitell 1986; Kohlberg 1971; Jones 1991; Rest 1994; Vitell and Muncy 2005). Less, yet still consistent, attention was given to country-of-origin, consumer ethnocentrism and cultural frameworks (testing for example the impact of Hofstede's cultural variables on consumers' intentions towards counterfeit and pirated goods), perceived risk theory (Bauer 1967) and luxury consumption theories (regarding for example Veblen 1899, concept of 'conspicuous consumption' or, more recently, Vigneron and Johnson's 2004 Luxury Brand Index, LBI). Scattered attention was given to brand-related theories (such as brand image, brand characteristics, brand imitation, brand confusion), self-related theories (self-identity, self-image, self-monitoring and self-presentation), social theories (social cognitive theory and social identity theory), criminology theories (neutralization and deterrence) utility theories, cognitive dissonance theory, equity theory and word-of-mouth.

The articles that have employed the above-mentioned frameworks are:

1) Attitude-intention models (*TRA*: Ang et al. 2001; De Matos et al. 2007; Wang et al. 2005; *TPB*: Cronan and Al-Rafee 2008; Penz and Stöttinger 2005; Yoon 2011; *Mixed*: Phau and Teah 2009; Chiou et al. 2005; Huang et al. 2004);
2) Ethical and moral decision making theories (*Ethical decision-making*: Lysonski and Durvasula 2008; Gopal and Sanders 1998; Wang et al. 2013; *Moral decision-making*: Swinyard et al. 1990; Kini et al. 2004; Logsdon et al. 1994; *Mixed*: Moores and Chang 2006; Husted and Allen 2008);
3) Country-of-origin and culture (Husted 2000; Wan et al. 2009; Chakraborty et al. 1996);
4) Perceived risk theory (Tan 2002; Veloutsou and Bian 2008; Sinha and Mandel 2008; Liao et al. 2010);
5) Luxury consumption theories (Nia and Zaichkowsky 2000; Juggessur and Cohen 2009; Han et al. 2010; Penz and Stöttinger 2012; Kapferer and Michaut 2014);
6) Other theories (from deterrence to neutralization theories, from equity to expected utility theory, from social identity and cognition to word-of-mouth) (Siponen et al. 2012; Glass and Wood 1996; Kuo and Hsu 2001; Chaudhry et al. 2011b; Lan et al. 2012).

These articles examined either overall consumer behavior with illicit goods (OCB) or delved into different typologies of antecedents to consumer attitudes, intentions and behaviors (Eisend and Schuchert-Güler 2006). They have been categorized as (Table 5.5):

a) *Personal factors* (PeF) (i.e. demographic variables, ethical ideologies, perceived risk);
b) *Product-related factors* (PrF) (i.e. price, quality, image);
c) *Social and cultural factors* (SoF) (i.e. informative and normative susceptibility, subjective norms, word-of-mouth);
d) *Situational factors* (SiF) (i.e. mood, context, hedonic shopping experience, availability).

Since previous studies on consumer behavior have mostly been single, stand-alone instances, what is currently missing in the literature is the further validation of results, through replication studies, in order to develop a generalizable model of consumer complicity valid across cultures and countries.

Table 5.5 Categories of CB articles, descriptions and variables

Category	Description	Determinants/variables
Overall consumer behavior (**OCB**)	Models analyzing overall attitudes, intentions and behaviors	Attitude, purchase intention, willingness to buy, willingness to try
Person and personality factors (**PeF**)	Individual characteristics in terms of demographic factors, psychographic factors and personality traits	Demographic variables (age, gender, income, education, occupation, marital status), value consciousness, integrity, personal gratification, perceived risks, self-image, fashion involvement, ethical ideologies, ethical judgment, materialism, moral intensity, moral equity, religious orientation
Product-related factors (**PrF**)	Characteristics of the counterfeit/pirated good, also in comparison to the original	Price, quality, brand image, retailer image, durability, style, product attributes, performance
Social and cultural factors (**SoF**)	Evaluations carried out by the individual in regards to their social and cultural sphere	Culture and cultural variables (collectivism/individualism, masculinity/femininity), country-of-origin, status consumption, informative and normative susceptibility, aspiration, subjective norms, word-of-mouth (WOM), social norms, perceived harm, peer pressure
Situational and contextual factors (**SiF**)	Purchase situations and contextual influences	Mood, purchase situation, hedonic shopping environment, novelty seeking, context, scarcity, shortage, purchase for oneself, purchase as a present for others, urgency, need

5.5 Supply-Side Investigations

Scarce is the literature addressing the supply of counterfeit and pirated goods. Papers in this category have mostly addressed the legitimate supply and distribution chains of original goods in markets with counterfeits (Bockstedt et al. 2006; Graham et al. 2004; Warr and Goode 2011; Olsen and Granzin 1992). Very few studies have addressed the illegal supply and distribution of counterfeit and pirated goods (Cartwright 2000; Goode and Cruise 2006; Walls and Harvey 2006; Staake et al. 2012; Stevenson and Busby 2015).

5.6 Anti-counterfeiting/Piracy Strategies, Tools and Actions

Different are the managerial responses suggested in the academic literature to combat counterfeiting and piracy.

The *early period* (1980–1993) is characterized by a first exploration into the possible solutions against counterfeiting and piracy. Researchers suggested a variety of strategies, from awareness to warning, from hands-off to withdrawal, from prosecution to assertion, (Kaikati and LaGarce 1980; Harvey and Ronkainen 1985; Harvey 1987). In the *development period* (1994–2003), scholars began to aggregate an already fragmented literature, suggesting strategies such as stakeholder education, coalitions, legislation, labeling and proactive marketing (Shultz II and Saporito 1996; Chaudhry and Walsh 1996; Krechevsky 2000; Jacobs et al. 2001; Hess 2003). Finally, in the *maturity period* (2004–2015), contributions on the managerial responses to counterfeiting and piracy have been consolidated, aggregated, accepted and—most of all—validated with managers, through either surveys (Yang et al. 2008), in-depth interviews (Keupp et al. 2010; Yang et al. 2004; Cesareo and Stöttinger 2015) or case studies (Casadesus-Masanell and Hervas-Drane 2010). Scholars suggested strategies such as proactive approaches, defensive weapons and networking means.

The tools employed in the fight against counterfeiting and piracy have been classified as: *track-and-trace technologies* (used to identify and track legitimate goods in the supply and distribution chains, such as authenticity cards and RFID labels), *covert technologies* (devices not visible to the naked-eye and detectable only by authorized personnel, such as watermarking and invisible inks) and *overt* technologies (detectable by everyone, including, final consumers, such as bar codes and microchip labels) (Li 2013; Berman 2008; Sudler 2013).

The multitude of strategies and tools suggested, often with conceptual and practical overlaps, highlights the need for an underpinning framework capable of synthesizing the plethora of existing strategic options into conceptually uniform and sound categories.

5.7 Conclusion

This chapter delved into the contents of the past 35 years of research on counterfeiting and piracy, highlighting six main categories, from consumer behavior to the managerial solutions, from international frameworks to the effects of the phenomena, from general descriptions to the supply analyses. We now tie in all the findings, descriptive and content, to highlight the main insights from the study, the managerial implications and discuss some of the most recent research that tries to tackle emerging gaps in the literature while proposing an agenda for future research in the field.

References

Ajzen I (1991) The theory of planned behavior. Organ Behav Hum Decis Process 50(2):179–211

Ang SH, Cheng PS, Lim EA, Tambyah SK (2001) Spot the difference: consumer responses towards counterfeits. J Consum Mark 18(3):219–235

Bauer R (1967) Consumer behavior as risk taking. In: Cox D (ed) Risk taking and information handling in consumer behavior. Harvard University Press, Cambridge, MA

Bender T (2006) How to cope with China's (alleged) failure to implement the TRIPS obligations on enforcement. J World Intellect Property 9(2):230–250

Berman B (2008) Strategies to detect and reduce counterfeiting activity. Bus Horiz 51(3):191–199

Bockstedt JC, Kauffman RJ, Riggins FJ (2006) The move to artist-led on-line music distribution: a theory-based assessment and prospects for structural changes in the digital music market. Int J Elect Commer 10(3):7–38

Cartwright SD (2000) Napster: a business in search of a viable model. J Bus Strategy 21(5):28–32

Casadesus-Masanell R, Hervas-Drane A (2010) Competing against online sharing. Manag Decis 48(8):1247–1260

Cesareo L, Stöttinger B (2015) United we stand, divided we fall: how firms can engage consumers in their fight against counterfeits. Bus Horiz 58(5):527–537.

Chakraborty G, Allred AT, Bristol T (1996) Exploring consumers' evaluations of counterfeits: the roles of country of origin and ethnocentrism. Adv Consum Res 23:379–384

Chaudhry PE (2006) Changing levels of intellectual property rights protection for global firms: a synopsis of recent US and EU trade enforcement strategies. Bus Horiz 49(6):463–472

Chaudhry PE, Walsh MG (1996) An assessment of the impact of counterfeiting in international markets: the piracy paradox persists. Columbia J World Bus 31(3):34–48

Chaudhry PE, Zimmerman A, Peters JR, Cordell VV (2009) Preserving intellectual property rights: managerial insight into the escalating counterfeit market quandary. Bus Horiz 52 (1):57–66

Chaudhry PE, Chaudhry SS, Stumpf SA, Sudler H (2011a) Piracy in cyber space: consumer complicity, pirates and enterprise enforcement. Enterp Inf Syst 5(2):255–271

Chaudhry PE, Hill RP, Stumpf SA, Yalcinkaya G (2011b) Consumer complicity across emerging markets. Adv Int Mark 22:223–239

Chen YN, Png I (2003) Information goods pricing and copyright enforcement: Welfare analysis. Inf Syst Res 14(1):107–123

Chiou JS, Huang CY, Lee HH (2005) The antecedents of music piracy attitudes and intentions. J Bus Ethics 57(2):161–174

Cronan TP, Al-Rafee S (2008) Factors that influence the intention to pirate software and media. J Bus Ethics 78(4):527–545

Das S, Mukhopadhyay A, Bagchi KK (2014) National-level determinants of global music piracy and online music sales: an exploratory study. J Global Inf Technol Manag 17(1):6–25

De Castro JO, Balkin DB, Shepherd DA (2007) Knock-off or knockout? Bus Strategy Rev 18 (1):28–32

De Matos CA, Ituassu CT, Rossi CAV (2007) Consumer attitudes toward counterfeits: a review and extension. J Consum Mark 24(1):36–47

Eisend M, Schuchert-Güler P (2006) Explaining counterfeit purchases: a review and preview. Acad Mark Sci Rev 12(6):1–25

Ferrante M (2015) China's renewed attention to the fight against counterfeit products sold online: the impact of Taobao's new policy and punishments. J Internet Law 3–10

Fishbein M, Ajzen I (1975) Belief, attitude, intention and behavior: an introduction to theory and research

Givon M, Mahajan V, Muller E (1995) Software piracy: estimation of lost sales and the impact on software diffusion. J Mark 29–37

Glass RS, Wood WA (1996) Situational determinants of software piracy: an equity theory perspective. J Bus Ethics 15(11):1189–1198

Goode S, Cruise S (2006) What motivates software crackers? J Bus Ethics 65(2):173–201
Gopal RD, Sanders GL (1998) International software piracy: analysis of key issues and impacts. Inf Syst Res 9(4):380–397
Gopal RD, Sanders GL (2000) Global software piracy: you can't get blood out of a turnip. Commun ACM 43(9):82–89
Graham G, Burnes B, Lewis GJ, Langer J (2004) The transformation of the music industry supply chain: a major label perspective. Int J Oper Prod Manag 24(11):1087–1103
Grassi I (2014) Cartel sustainability and piracy in a vertically differentiated oligopoly. Rev Econ Res 11(1):9–31
Grossman GM, Shapiro C (1988) Foreign counterfeiting of status goods
Han JY, Nunes JC, and Drèze X (2010) Signaling status with luxury goods: the role of brand prominence. J Market 74(4):15–30
Harvey MG (1987) Industrial product counterfeiting: problems and proposed solutions. J Bus Ind Mark 2(4):5–13
Harvey MG, Ronkainen IA (1985) International counterfeiters-marketing success without the cost and the risk. Columbia J World Bus 20(3):37–45
Hennig-Thurau T, Henning V, Sattler H (2007) Consumer file sharing of motion pictures. J Mark 71(4):1–18
Hess, GM (2003) Combating online software piracy. J Internet Commerce, 2(3):3–10
Huang JH, Lee BC, Ho SH (2004) Consumer attitude toward gray market goods. Int Mark Rev 21 (6):598–614
Hunt SD, Vitell S (1986) A general theory of marketing ethics. J Macromarketing 6(1):5–16
Husted BW (2000) The impact of national culture on software piracy. J Bus Ethics 26(3):197–211
Husted BW, Allen DB (2008) Toward a model of cross-cultural business ethics: The impact of individualism and collectivism on the ethical decision-making process. J Bus Ethics 82 (2):293–305
Jacobs L, Samli AC, Jedlik T (2001) The nightmare of international product piracy: exploring defensive strategies. Ind Mark Manage 30(6):499–509
Jain SC (1996) Problems in international protection of intellectual property rights. J Int Mark 4 (1):9–32
Jandhyala S (2015) International and domestic dynamics of intellectual property protection. J World Bus 50(2):284–293
Jones TM (1991) Ethical decision making by individuals in organizations: an issue-contingent model. Acad Manag Rev 16(2):366–395
Juggessur J, Cohen G (2009) Is fashion promoting counterfeit brands? J Brand Manag 16(5):383–394
Kaikati JG, LaGarce R (1980) Beware of international brand piracy. Harvard Bus Rev 58(2):52
Kapferer JN, Michaut A (2014) Luxury counterfeit purchasing: the collateral effect of luxury brands' trading down policy. J Brand Strategy 3(1):59–70
Keupp APMM, Beckenbauer PCA, Gassmann O (2010) Enforcing intellectual property rights in weak appropriability regimes. Manag Int Rev 50(1):109–130
Kini RB, Ramakrishna HV, Vijayaraman BS (2004) Shaping of moral intensity regarding software piracy: a comparison between Thailand and US students. J Bus Ethics 49(1):91–104
Koh B, Murthi BPS, Raghunathan S (2014) Shifting demand: online music piracy, physical music sales, and digital music sales. J Org Comput Elect Commer 24(4):366–387
Kohlberg L (1971) Stages of moral development. Moral Educ 23–92
Kopp SW, Suter TA (2000) Trademark strategies online: implications for intellectual property protection. J Pub Policy Mark 19(1):119–131
Krechevsky C (2000) The multinational approach to anti-counterfeiting. J of Proprietary Rights 12 (9):1–12
Kuo FY, Hsu MH (2001) Development and validation of ethical computer self-efficacy measure: the case of softlifting. J Bus Ethics 32(4):299–315
Lan MY, Liu F, Fang CH, Lin TM (2012) Understanding word-of-mouth in counterfeiting. Psychology 3(03):289

Li L (2013) Technology designed to combat fakes in the global supply chain. Bus Horiz 56 (2):167–177

Liao C, Lin HN, Liu YP (2010) Predicting the use of pirated software: a contingency model integrating perceived risk with the theory of planned behavior. J Bus Ethics 91(2):237–252

Liebowitz, SJ (2006) File Sharing: Creative Destruction or Just Plain Destruction?*. J Law Econ 49(1):1–28

Logsdon JM, Thompson JK, Reid RA (1994) Software piracy: is it related to level of moral judgment? J Bus Ethics 13(11):849–857

Lunney GS (2001) The death of copyright: digital technology, private copying, and the digital millennium copyright act. Virginia Law Rev 813–920

Lysonski S, Durvasula S (2008) Digital piracy of MP3s: consumer and ethical predispositions. J Consum Mark 25(3):167–178

Ma L, Montgomery AL, Singh PV, Smith MD (2014) An empirical analysis of the impact of pre-release movie piracy on box office revenue. Inf Syst Res 25(3):590–603

Moores TT, Chang JCJ (2006) Ethical decision making in software piracy: initial development and test of a four-component model. Mis Q 167–180

Nia A, Zaichkowsky JL (2000) Do counterfeits devalue the ownership of luxury brands? J Prod Brand Manag 9(7):485–497

Nill A, Shultz CJ II (1996) The scourge of global counterfeiting. Bus Horiz 39(6):37–42

Nill A, Shultz CJ II (2009) Global software piracy: trends and strategic considerations. Bus Horiz 52(3):289–298

Novos I, Waldman M (2013) Piracy of intellectual property: past, present, and future. Rev Econ Res 10(2):1–26

Oberholzer-Gee F, Strumpf K (2010) File sharing and copyright. In: Innovation policy and the economy, vol 10. University of Chicago Press, pp 19–55

Olsen JE, Granzin KL (1992) Gaining retailers assistance in fighting counterfeiting-conceptualization and empirical-test of a helping model. J Retail 68(1):90–109

Payne RW (2014) Unauthorized online dealers of "genuine" products in the amazon marketplace and beyond: remedies for brand owners. J Internet Law 3–9

Peitz M, Waelbroeck P (2006) Why the music industry may gain from free downloading—the role of sampling. Int J Ind Organ 24(5):907–913

Penz E, Stöttinger B (2005) Forget the "real" thing-take the copy! an explanatory model for the volitional purchase of counterfeit products. Adv Consum Res 32:568

Penz E, Stöttinger B (2012) A comparison of the emotional and motivational aspects in the purchase of luxury products versus counterfeits. J Brand Manag 19(7):581–594

Phau I, Teah M (2009) Devil wears (counterfeit) Prada: a study of antecedents and outcomes of attitudes towards counterfeits of luxury brands. J Consum Mark 26(1):15–27

Qian Y (2014a) Brand management and strategies against counterfeits. J Econ Manag Strategy 23 (2):317–343

Qian Y (2014b) Counterfeiters: foes or friends? How counterfeits affect sales by product quality tier. Manage Sci 60(10):2381–2400

Rest JR (1994) Background: theory and research. Moral Dev Prof: Psychol Appl Ethics 1–26

Roy A (2007) A new dispute concerning the TRIPS agreement: the United States and China in the WTO. J World Intellect Property 10(6):476–484

Scott CD (2013) Trademark strategy in the internet age: customer hijacking and the doctrine of initial interest confusion. J Retail 89(2):176–189

Shultz CJ II, Saporito B (1996) Protecting intellectual property: strategies and recommendations to deter counterfeiting and brand piracy in global markets. Columbia J World Bus 31(1):18–28

Sinha RK, Mandel N (2008) Preventing digital music piracy: the carrot or the stick? J Mark 72 (1):1–15

Siponen M, Vance A, Willison R (2012) New insights into the problem of software piracy: the effects of neutralization, shame, and moral beliefs. Inf Manag 49(7):334–341

Smith MD, Telang R (2009) Competing with free: the impact of movie broadcasts on DVD sales and internet piracy 1. MIS Q 33(2):321–338

Staake T, Thiesse F, Fleisch E (2009) The emergence of counterfeit trade: a literature review. Eur J Mark 43(3/4):320–349. doi:10.1108/03090560910935451
Staake T, Thiesse F, Fleisch E (2012) Business strategies in the counterfeit market. J Bus Res 65 (5):658–665
Stevenson M, Busby J (2015) An exploratory analysis of counterfeiting strategies: towards counterfeit-resilient supply chains. Int J Oper Prod Manag 35(1):110–144
Sudler H (2013) Effectiveness of anti-piracy technology: finding appropriate solutions for evolving online piracy. Bus Horiz 56(2):149–157
Swinyard WR, Rinne H, Kau AK (1990) The morality of software piracy: a cross-cultural analysis. J Bus Ethics 9(8):655–664
Takeyama LN (1994) The welfare implications of unauthorized reproduction of intellectual property in the presence of demand network externalities. J Ind Econ 155–166
Tan B (2002) Understanding consumer ethical decision making with respect to purchase of pirated software. J Consum Mark 19(2):96–111
Thurow, LC (1997) Needed: a new system of intellectual property rights. Harvard Bus Rev 75:94–107
Van Eecke P, & Truyens M (2008) Recent Events in EU Internet Law, J Internet Law, 4:28–29
Veblen T (1899) The theory of the leisure class. Am Lib, New York
Veloutsou C, Bian X (2008) A cross-national examination of consumer perceived risk in the context of non-deceptive counterfeit brands. J Consum Behav 7(1):3–20
Vigneron F, Johnson LW (2004) Measuring perceptions of brand luxury. J Brand Manag 11 (6):484–506
Vitell SJ, Muncy J (2005) The Muncy–Vitell consumer ethics scale: a modification and application. J Bus Ethics 62(3):267–275
Walls WD, Harvey PJ (2006) Digital pirates in practice: analysis of market transactions in Hong Kong's pirate software arcades. Int J Manag 23(2):207–214
Wan WW, Luk CL, Yau OH, Alan CB, Sin LY, Kwong KK, Chow RP (2009) Do traditional Chinese cultural values nourish a market for pirated CDs? J Bus Ethics 88(1):185–196
Wang F, Zhang H, Zang H, Ouyang M (2005) Purchasing pirated software: an initial examination of Chinese consumers. J Consum Mark 22(6):340–351
Wang YS, Yeh CH, Liao YW (2013) What drives purchase intention in the context of online content services? The moderating role of ethical self-efficacy for online piracy. Int J Inf Manag 33(1):199–208
Warr R, Goode MM (2011) Is the music industry stuck between rock and a hard place? The role of the Internet and three possible scenarios. J Retail Consum Serv 18(2):126–131
Wilke R, Zaichkowsky JL (1999) Brand imitation and its effects on innovation, competition, and brand equity. Bus Horiz 42(6):9–18
Yang D, Clarke P (2005) Globalisation and intellectual property in China. Technovation 25 (5):545–555
Yang D, Sonmez M, Bosworth D (2004) Intellectual property abuses: how should multinationals respond? Long Range Plan 37(5):459–475
Yang D, Fryxell GE, Sie AK (2008) Anti-piracy effectiveness and managerial confidence: insights from multinationals in China. J World Bus 43(3):321–339
Yoon C (2011) Theory of planned behavior and ethics theory in digital piracy: an integrated model. J Bus Ethics 100(3):405–417
Zentner A (2005) File sharing and international sales of copyrighted music: an empirical analysis with a panel of countries. Topics Econ Anal Policy 5(1):1–15

Chapter 6
Discussion, Managerial Implications, Current and Future Research

Abstract The purpose of this chapter is to join the findings from the descriptive and content analyses in order to highlight the main insights from the study, the managerial implications and discuss some of the most recent research that tries to tackle emerging gaps in the literature while proposing an agenda for future research in the field.

Keywords Insights · Managerial implications · Findings · New research · Future research

From the descriptive and content analyses carried out on the selected articles, different are the insights, the managerial implications and the gaps in the literature. After summarizing the key findings, the Author puts forth some of the most recent research that tackles different gaps identified in the literature while suggesting future paths for both research and practice.

6.1 Insights from the Descriptive Analysis

First of all, the fact that the first contributions to the literature (1980–1990) were mostly theoretical (Sect. 4.1) can be explained as a need to first delve into the phenomena from a conceptual perspective in order to define the scope, study the underlying dimensions and mechanisms, and understand the main actors involved. As more and more was known and pulled out, empirical validations of conceptual frameworks became the major focus of academics worldwide.

In terms of Authorship (Sect. 4.2), while the prevalence of American and European authors is evident, analyzing the trends over time highlights how, with the beginning of the 21st century and the shift in the global economic equilibrium towards newly industrialized countries (i.e. BRICs), authorship of papers on counterfeiting and piracy has also shifted, mostly towards Asian and Middle-Eastern contributors. While this increasing focus on developing economies is encouraging because it is better representative of the global population for which

L. Cesareo, *Counterfeiting and Piracy*,
SpringerBriefs in Business, DOI 10.1007/978-3-319-25357-2_6

counterfeiting is an issue, there remains a need for more research on the so-called BRIC countries (Brazil, Russia, India, China) where the problem is largest and most persistent.

In terms of distribution channels (Sect. 4.4), the literature again follows the real-life context: the advent of the Internet, of digital technologies, of P2P networks and of file sharing services has pushed authors to study this new, pervasive and shoreless distribution channel that causes major headaches to managers worldwide. The fact that traditional channels have been complemented by digital, online channels, calls for greater research into the combined online and offline distribution of counterfeit and pirated goods worldwide.

In terms of industries and product categories analyzed (Sect. 4.5), the results highlight the prevalence of studies on software and music in terms of intellectual products and copyright violations, and on luxury and fashion goods in terms of physical products and trademark violations. Therefore, instead of further delving into these industries by replicating prior models slightly tweaked to modify just one or two antecedents, the literature should concentrate on other industries and product categories, such as pharmaceuticals and auto-parts, since these have, for example, tragic consequences upon their often unaware users.

Looking into the empirical studies (Sects. 4.1.1.1 and 4.1.1.2), the first result that stands out regards the data-collection methods: surveys in quantitative research (80.8 %) and in-depth interviews in qualitative research (63.3 %) dominate the scenario. Since counterfeiting and piracy are illegal, unethical acts and consumers perceive them as such, their responses are often biased to adjust to socially desirable conducts while not reflecting their actual attitudes, intentions and behaviors. Therefore, there is a great need to go beyond self-reported measures and obtain more unbiased responses, derived from either real-life experiments or natural observations.

In terms of sampling, the results highlight how there is a great number of student samples in quantitative studies (53.1 %) and a majority of adult consumer samples in qualitative studies (78.3 %). While part of the literature agrees that students are an appropriate sample for counterfeiting and piracy studies (given their demographic characteristics and their natural propensity towards these products due to specific psychographic characteristics), the results found amongst this social group cannot be generalized to the broader public. In addition, consumers are mostly surveyed in developed markets (e.g., USA) that have less counterfeit and pirated goods compared to some developing markets (e.g. Southeast Asia). Furthermore, the fact that regression and SEM are the most used methods of analysis, highlights how the level of statistical sophistication has greatly improved. Clearly, there is a need for a more thorough quantitative examination of adult consumer samples in markets replete with counterfeit and pirated goods, such as China, Taiwan and Hong Kong, and the use of multiple methodologies of analysis. The shift in Authorship could help in filling this void.

6.2 Insights from the Content Analysis

Looking at the article categories, the first result that stands out is the staggering prevalence of demand-side investigations (46.0 %) compared to all other categories, and the few supply-side investigations (10.4 %). Even if obtaining information on the infringers' activities is a very hard task, further understanding the supply of counterfeit and pirated goods, in terms of supply and distribution chains, both offline and online, and the underlying processes could be of vital help to managers and governments engaged in the fight against them. For these reasons, this field should get more attention from scholars in the near future.

While the literature commonly claims the need for more consumer analyses, what is actually evident is that the plethora of studies on different theoretical underpinnings and consumption behavior models available often lack substantial differences. Testing models that add or remove single determinants, define identical variables differently and change the scope of the analyses cannot be considered substantive additions to the literature. What is currently missing, and therefore needed, is: (1) the development and validation of a generalizable model of consumer complicity across a substantial number of countries and cultures that is representative of the phenomenon; and (2) the study of consumer acceptance of legal alternatives to counterfeiting and piracy, both offline and online.

To address the first issue, the Author and two Colleagues developed and tested a general model of consumer complicity with counterfeit goods across five country markets (BRIC and the United States). The results are highly interesting and they signify the common characteristics of complicit consumers across country markets (low ethical concern, search for a hedonic shopping experience, high perceived quality) (Chaudhry et al. 2014).

To address the second issue, the Author and a Colleague delved into consumers' attitudes and behaviors towards online music piracy and a possible legal alternative (subscription-based music services—SBMS). The results show how a favorable attitude toward online piracy (positively influenced by economic and hedonic benefits and negatively by moral judgment) negatively influences consumers' willingness to try SBMS. These findings suggest that music industry actors need to increase their commitment and educate consumers about the consequences and implications of online music piracy, while also stressing the value added and hedonic benefits offered by SBMS (Cesareo and Pastore 2014a).

Another category well analyzed in the literature is the managerial responses to counterfeiting and piracy (12.3 %): many studies have addressed companies' strategies, tools and actions against these instances, often repeating and categorizing differently similar solutions. Research should therefore focus its attention towards: (1) delving into the managerial perceptions of the causes of the phenomena in order to develop a brand protection/anti-counterfeiting/piracy framework that can synthesize existing strategies and actions into general guidelines of practical help for managers; and (2) studying the perceived effectiveness of anti-counterfeiting/piracy strategies, tools and actions from a consumer perspective, in order to maximize managerial efforts and results.

To address the former issue, the Author worked with a Colleague by joining the suggestions from the literature with practical, real-life solutions employed by companies worldwide. After extensive, in-depth interviews with managers, the proposed final brand protection, anti-counterfeiting framework consists of four strategies: *protection*, *collaboration*, *prosecution* and *information* (for a detailed explanation of each strategy refer to Cesareo and Pastore 2014b; Pastore and Cesareo 2014).

To address the latter issue, the Author is currently working with two Colleagues to understand consumer perceptions regarding the effectiveness of anti-counterfeiting/piracy strategies. The hope is that such an understanding will contribute to strengthen companies' efforts in developing effective campaigns and initiatives that can really tackle consumer demand for counterfeit and pirated goods worldwide.

References

Cesareo L, Pastore A (2014a) Consumers' attitude and behavior towards online music piracy and subscription-based services. J Consum Mark 31(6/7):515–525

Cesareo L, Pastore A (2014b) Acting on luxury counterfeiting. In: Reinecke S, Berghaus B, Mueller-Stewens G (eds) The management of luxury. Kogan Page, USA, pp 341–359

Chaudhry PE, Cesareo L, Stumpf SA (2014) What influences rampant movie piracy? J Manag Syst 24(4):73–95

Pastore A, Cesareo L (2014) No al falso! Un'indagine esplorativa sulle strategie anti-contraffazione delle fashion firms. Mercati e Competitività 2:81–102

Chapter 7
Conclusion

Abstract The purpose of this chapter is to sum up the main contributions of this book and offer suggestions about the future of the counterfeiting and piracy literature by providing some paths for the further developments of these fields.

Keywords Contribution · Future research · Online counterfeiting · Consumer acceptance · Piracy

This book examined the evolution of research on counterfeiting and piracy in the period 1980–2015 by content analyzing academic articles published in multi-disciplinary journals.

Two were the main objectives: (1) analyze the current state-of-the-art on the counterfeiting and piracy phenomena, highlighting the main trends in terms of methodologies employed, samples used, distribution channels and products tested; and (2) categorize existing research based upon emerging themes in order to draw insights on under-researched areas that should be further delved into in the future.

From a methodological perspective, the research offers itself to some limitations that suggest challenges and guidelines for further development. First, the inclusion of only scholarly journal articles (even if they constitute the most numerous contributions on the topics) and the omission of other sources (such as books, book chapters and trade publications) might have biased the results of the literature review. Second, the broad number of journals included and the fact that they belong to diverse disciplinary areas, while giving a good overview of the phenomena does not leave room for deep insights into single areas. A further analysis could study scholarly articles published, for example, in only the 'marketing' or 'business and management' fields to profoundly delve into the contributions of scholars within a single field. Finally, given the high number of articles analyzed, while the qualitative content analysis and related descriptive statistics offer some suggestive insights, they could be further implemented by a quantitative content analysis or a meta-analysis.

Academic research on counterfeiting and piracy has gained momentum over the past decade, yet there remains substantial room for further academic inquiry: from the validation of a general model of consumer complicity, valid across cultures and

L. Cesareo, *Counterfeiting and Piracy*,
SpringerBriefs in Business, DOI 10.1007/978-3-319-25357-2_7

demographics, to the analysis of consumer acceptance of legal alternatives to counterfeiting and piracy across different domains; from the understanding of managerial perceptions of the phenomena to the development of *ad hoc*, internet-based solutions to the widespread phenomenon of online deception.

The Author hopes to have spurred the reader's interest and signified the importance of studying counterfeiting and piracy in order to foster a more proactive fight against such illicit instances.

The manufacturer's authorised representative in the EU is Springer Nature Customer Service Centre GmbH, Europaplatz 3, 69115 Heidelberg, Germany. If you have any concerns regarding our products, please contact ProductSafety@springernature.com

Printed and bound by CPI Group (UK) Ltd, Croydon, CR0 4YY
25/09/2026
02222857-0014